In Fight for It, Roger Patterson very best efforts to advance t around us. Drawing on the wisdom of Scripture, inspiring and helpful advice, this book is a must-read for anyone who wants to make a difference for Christ!

−D. MICHAEL LINDSAY, author, Hinge Moments;
president, Taylor University

Roger Patterson has written an authentic and scripturally thoughtful book, one that has challenged me to ask basic questions about things that really matter: my personal devotion to Christ, my family, and the witness of the church. In all these arenas, there is soul-searching to do and habits to change so that we exercise the influence in the world that God has called us to have. I gladly commend this book.

−DR. ROBERT SLOAN, President, Houston Baptist University

Has life knocked you down? Have you gotten hit by a combination of punches? Are you constantly bobbing and weaving, desperately avoiding the swings of your enemy, unsure of whether you can handle another blow? ... The good news is that you don't have to stay on the defensive. You don't have to lose. Victory is yours. In Fight for It, Pastor Roger Patterson teaches you how to lay hold of the win that Christ has already given you.

−CHRIS BROUSSARD, Sports Broadcaster and NBA Analyst, Founder/
President of The K.I.N.G. Movement

In Fight for It, Roger Patterson has brought out truth that is profoundly important for the time in which we live. Drawn from the pages of Scripture, Roger's work does more than motivate Christians to do more; this content gives them a new way of looking at the challenges ahead and experiencing victory in their own "Fight Stories."

−RYAN RUSH, Founder of Empowered Homes &
Senior Pastor, Kingsland Baptist Church

Roger Patterson is a leader of leaders. This excellent study reminds us that there are some fights that are worth the effort. Mining the stories of Ezra and Nehemiah, Roger points us toward a great future for our families and our churches. God will use this book to help us move forward together.

Many of us spend life wondering when the "stroll in the park" section begins. Unfortunately life is more of a fight than a stroll. But good news… God is with you and Roger has written "Fight for It" to show the path of winning in Christ. His book and the accompanying resources shine with great news… God has a plan for your battle and He is fighting for you! "Fight for It" is an effective tool for discovering, reminding and walking in the fight, victoriously. Read it to win.

I've been in a few fights in my life – from fighting for a World Series to fighting through addiction – I know that in so many ways, life is a fight. In Fight For It, Pastor Roger Patterson helps us understand four key fights for every follower of Jesus Christ. Keep fighting…

Roger Patterson has so well identified and addressed one of the greatest needs in our world. The need to FIGHT for what we believe in. Thankfully, he also included Biblical strategies to do so. Fight for It is rich with content and wisdom that is vital to navigate the challenges of life.

You can't win, unless you know what you're fighting against. You can't be victorious until you know how not to lose-this new book uniquely speaks to the challenge and opportunity we all have to battle for everyday-and how to win! I'm thankful for its wisdom for life's daily match!

"Fight for It" is a call to action encouraging us to recognize the things in life that are truly worth our time, focus, energy and prayer. In other words, the things that are worth fighting for. Dr. Roger Patterson provides sound biblical teaching and innovative resources in this thought-provoking read. He has a way of igniting fresh understanding using simple illustrations to clarify deep spiritual truths. I know we will all be blessed by this teaching on how a "good fight" can strengthen marriages, heal homes, fortify the church, and even influence culture.

—**DR. ED YOUNG,** Senior Pastor, Second Baptist Church, Houston

If you're like me, you've gotten knocked down by life sometime during the last couple of years. That's why I was so excited to see Roger Patterson's work in Fight For It. He takes clear principles from one of my favorite books on rebuilding (Nehemiah) and applies them to today's challenges. You've either been knocked down, or you will be. Either way, you need this book.

-**WILLIAM VANDERBLOEMEN,** Founder and CEO Vanderbloemen

The books of Ezra and Nehemiah present one of the most unexpected comeback stories in history. They tell of the amazing impact of ordinary people, led by God, to dream the extraordinary. "Fight for it" skillfully weaves our everyday choices and challenges into the narrative and demonstrates how we too can be used by God to impact not only the lives of our family but the lives of our city. It pushes us to dream bigger.

-**DR. MARK HARTMAN,** Lead Pastor, Sugar Creek Baptist Church

Leaders should expect struggle and learn how to power through.Knowing what fights lay ahead, and that some fights matter while others don't, are critical junctures in the journey of every leader. This book will be a great resource for any who are seeking to use God's word for counsel, discernment, and encouragement as they navigate the fights that truly are worth fighting.

-**DR. JOSH ELLIS,** Executive Director UBA, Houston

FIGHT FOR IT

WHAT IN YOUR LIFE IS WORTH FIGHTING FOR?

ROGER PATTERSON

CityRise
Houston, Texas

Table of Contents

Introduction

And I looked and arose and said to the nobles and to the officials and to the rest of the people, "Do not be afraid of them. Remember the Lord, who is great and awesome, and fight for your brothers, your sons, your daughters, your wives, and your homes."

Nehemiah 4:14, ESV

I finally reached the last exercise of the 30-minute training session. I hadn't been in the gym in a while, and I was excited to lace my shoes back up and take a step forward. I was also nervous. I hadn't been pushing myself physically for many months. I was in an overwhelming season and feeling defeated. I was ready to quit the pastorate and sell popcorn—anything, frankly, if I could put this season in the rear-view mirror.

As Brent Gallagher, owner of Avenu Fitness and Lifestyle, pulled the battle-rope off the wall, he demonstrated the movement I was to do then handed me the ends. He hit the button on his stopwatch to initiate this quick hitting interval training. The first movement wasn't that bad, as I handled the rope well for 20 seconds and then took a 20 second break. During that time, he showed me the next movement and I got after it —20 seconds of movement and 20 seconds of rest.

At the third move, he said, "Okay, let's take this rope. I want you to slam it up and down as many times as possible, as high as you can, as hard as you can." He then proceeded to slam the rope to demonstrate. Like the two previous movements, I was game to grab the rope and slam it out. I was eager to perform for him, as he was making an investment in me. He and his wife Cassie knew some of the journey this season had required, as our church went through a tough season together, and this training session was a gift to get me moving in the right direction.

As I grabbed the rope this third time and stood tall with a solid base, Brent put his thumb on the start button of his watch and said, "And Roger, if there is anything inside you that needs to come out, get it out right now and leave it here." To this, I replied, "Okay, sounds good."

My reply was from a place of ignorance. Had I known what would come next, I would have said, "Hey, thanks for the workout. Those 29 minutes and 40 seconds were great. Maybe we will do this again." But those last 20 seconds changed my life. Those last 20 seconds showed me I was in a fight, and I was losing. It was time to rise up from a place of defeat and fight for my future.

Has life knocked you down? Have you gotten hit by a combination of punches? Are you running and ducking because you just don't know if you can handle another blow? It's a devastating place to feel so defeated when your Bible, your small group, even your favorite preacher says you are more than a conqueror.

CAN 20 SECONDS CHANGE YOUR LIFE TOO?

I still haven't gotten over that final rope slam. In that 20 second slam, I began to slam out all that I was carrying inside of me. As I slammed that rope over and over again, the weight of pain, grief, and loss began to well up from the bottom of my heels, through my midsection, up through my throat, and out of my tear ducts. As I continued to slam that rope, I heard the Holy Spirit say to me, "Roger, you've got some work to do." Tears flowed, my chest heaved for breath, and I turned my head in embarrassment. Little did I know that the God of the universe would call to me in a gym in the heart of Houston, Texas.

This was an invitation from bondage of my circumstances to a place of liberty and rejuvenation. This was an opportunity to look at the pain and grief I was dealing with squarely in the face and freely admit the toll it had on me. Weighing in at 306 pounds, knowing that I was on an unsustainable path, I had a choice to make. Would I continue as a victim of my circumstance, or would I put the mess into the hands of my Savior and allow Him to give me a message? I could stay down in defeat, fake it until I made it on my own, and fizz out somewhere along the way, or I could learn how to fight for my future.

LEARNING TO FIGHT

As you look around our world today on the macro-level, things are a mess. Our nation's healthcare system has been stretched to its limit. Our education system had to reinvent itself. The political landscape is deeply fractured. The country is divided right down the middle on which way we should head. On the micro-level, we have isolated from our neighbors. Our trust in leaders seems to be at an all-time low. We are tired, frazzled, at our limits. We wonder if things will ever return to normal.

Yet all these facts and feelings do not negate the reality that we have great potential as a people. Our story is not too dissimilar to what happened in the divided nations of Israel and Judah beginning in 605 B.C.

Many were asking, "Where did we go wrong?" Others asked, "Is there a way forward?" In this context—where the temple of the Lord, the walls of the city of Jerusalem, the hearts of the residents of the land, were lying in ruin—this is where God was up to something.

Before we dig into this story and learn about what God was up to, let me ask you some key questions to consider. In a sentence, can you clearly articulate:

- For what are you fighting?
- For whom are you fighting?
- What do you believe is worthy of your fight?

Before I go another sentence into this work, please let me say what I am not advocating for—a political party or a political candidate. That's not the fight I am talking about. As a matter of fact, some of what I will be sharing with you is going to be counter-intuitive to the American way of fighting. This may please you or this may frustrate you. But I would ask that you hear me out. For way too long, we have focused on who is in the White House believing that person or party is going to "save" our way of life. We are looking for top-down solutions when our greatest abilities to author change come from the bottom-up. Like you, I certainly prefer what I want in a political leader and what I want in my party's platform. But that is not the direction I am headed. Instead, I want to tell you what I see in you and in the Scripture. You see, I see so much untapped potential for good for our homes and communities. Regardless of who is in office, we can pursue a peaceful future.

To unlock this potential, I want to begin by sharing two core convictions. The first is that you are a person of influence. You can affect what happens in your home and in your world through the unique abilities that God has given to you. You have talents that are needed in others' lives. You have treasure that has been entrusted to you. You have a skill set that your children's school needs. Your influence is the totality of your life experience up to this point, encompassing your various capacities, your financial means and the story you are writing in your relationships in the marketplace, at your university, or in your home.

We can use influence for good or for bad. We can use it to lift others, or we can use it to build up ourselves while we tear others down. We can exalt others, or we can pull them down. That's the power of influence.

The second conviction is that we are in a fight. It's a fight, as I said earlier, not for who occupies an office, but whether the one who rules and reigns over every office will have his way in our lives, our homes, our churches, and in our cities. Unless we know what it is we are fighting for, who we are fighting for, and what we believe is worth fighting for, we won't pay the price necessary to win the fight. Instead, we will stay busy with a sense that we are contributing to "something" but not have a clear view of what a win really looks like. So, again, let me ask, in a sentence, can you clearly articulate:

- For what are you fighting?
- For whom are you fighting?
- What do you believe is worthy of your fight?

Now, before you fully answer these three questions, I want to plant a seed with you. Naturally, we will answer the first two questions with how they relate to ourselves. We would say, "I'm fighting for myself, my home, for my marriage, for my children." Good! We must fight for ourselves and our homes. But what if we expanded the fight a bit? One of the primary ways we win at home is by growing in our faith. So, if we are going to battle for our futures, shouldn't we also fight for the long-term success of our church?

In the church, we are standing on the shoulders of generations who have gone before us and yet, like no other time in history, our churches have been severely impacted by the COVID-19 pandemic. When every other crisis has hit, people have flocked to the church. Yet in this recent crisis, people have scattered from the church.

Alan Platt, in his book City Changers, conveys that the church in the community is to have a fathering presence, a faithful presence and a fruitful presence.[1] His message is that the church has a critical role to play in society helping shepherd people's lives, demonstrating long-standing faithfulness, and bearing fruit whose benefits are far-reaching. Given the fact that many churches are still trying to reclaim many of their members and attenders from the COVID-19 lockdowns, and many churches went an entire year or more without knowing how effective they were in reaching new people, the reality for church leaders is that we know that we are in a fight for our influence in our own congregations' lives like never before. Will you fight for your church?

Now, before you say, "Okay, I know that I am fighting for myself, my home, and my church family," let's broaden our view to the role that followers of Jesus Christ are to play in our communities. Jesus called us salt and light; the city set upon a hill. Clearly, we are seen by Christ as influencers and understanding this helps us better understand why we gather to worship and fight for ourselves and our homes in the first place. The call of Jesus Christ is to penetrate the highways and byways with his Kingdom on earth as it is in heaven. Gathering for worship and leading our families in the things of God isn't so we will hide our developing characters and influence under a bowl. Instead, it's to light up the city and allow our light to shine before others, so they might find the hope that we have. You see, whether we see it or not, we are in a fight for our communities and our cities. In our homes and in our churches, we discover and develop the influence that Jesus puts in us all for the task of deploying that influence for His purpose and glory.

What could God do in a city where followers of Jesus rally to fight for themselves, their homes, the church, and the well-being of the city? If you don't read another word of this book, grasp this—it is through the influence of followers of Jesus that our lives, homes, churches, and cities will rise. But now, I am getting ahead of myself.

Let's step back in history a bit. Beginning in 605 B.C., the people of the nation of Israel experienced the hostile take-over of their nation by the Babylonian empire. This was the year that the Babylonians began to invade and deport people back to Babylon. You may recall names like Daniel, Shadrach, Meshach and Abednego. These were some of the best and brightest who were placed into the king's service. By 587 B.C., the great capital city of the southern kingdom of Judah fell. Jerusalem's walls were torn down, Solomon's grand temple was destroyed, and a small remnant remained in this once glorious, thriving city where David had been king.

This Babylonian captivity, as prophesied by Jeremiah, lasted a period of 70 years. The word of the Lord that came to the people through Jeremiah must have caught them by surprise. He told them, as captives, as an exiled people, to, "Seek the welfare of the city where I have sent you into exile, and pray to the Lord on it's behalf; for in its welfare you will have welfare," (Jeremiah 29:7, NASB).

Now, as Alan Platt, in his book, City Changers declares so well:

"To the people of Israel, Babylon was everything Jerusalem was not. Babylon was dedicated to false gods, while Jerusalem was dedicated to the one true God. Babylon was the center of pagan worship; Jerusalem hosted the only holy worship. Babylon was characterized by sin, while Jerusalem was the home of those worshippers blessed to love God's holy hill, where the ark of the covenant resided and where Solomon's temple towered over the city. Jerusalem was God's preferred address on Earth."[2]

What was God up to? What was He working out in His people? What was He trying to teach them? Why would He challenge them to seek the peace of…the welfare of…the good of the city of evil captors? Why would God call His people to seek the "Shalom" of her captor's home base?

The Scripture shows us that God had a much longer view than those stuck in exile. As a matter of fact, during this exile the prophecies of Daniel were recorded. During this exile Queen Esther saved the Jews. During this exile God was ridding Israel and Judah of her idolatry. During this time God was going to prepare a remnant to return to re-build Jerusalem. During this exile God was going to burden a king and raise up leaders to once again, make a city rise. That's the story of the Old Testament books of Ezra and Nehemiah.

When you study the story of Ezra and Nehemiah as they are in the Hebrew Bible, one and the same book, you find at least four big fights for which the followers of Jesus are also fighting. These fights of the saints of old challenge us and encourage us in our fight stories. In these, we see what it takes for an individual, a family, a church, or a city to rise off the mat of ruin and rebuild. As we study this story of the men and women who saw a brighter tomorrow, let's ask ourselves, how can we rebuild what's been torn down and find a peaceful future?

Before we go any further, I want to ask you to take a minute to reflect on your life, your home, your church, and your city. Take a minute to answer the questions below and think about your unique influence and what God may be stirring in you to rise, rebuild, and fight for your future.

REFLECTION QUESTIONS:

1. For what are you fighting? Describe what it is you believe you are fighting for each day.

2. For whom are you fighting? List each of them by name and what you hope for them.

3. What do you believe is worthy of your fight?

4. If you were to expand your fight beyond your home, would you see your church's long-term health and well-being as something worthy of your efforts?

5. Beyond your home and your church, what is one area of concern that you have for your city?

6. Given your concern for the city, do you even know where to begin to help influence it for good?

7. In the space provided below, record any other thoughts that you have considering your answers above.

SECTION 1

Fighting for Yourself: Avoid Crumbling in the Fight

"Something's happening!" Have you ever used that phrase? Maybe you were out on a bike ride, or you passed through a community, and you saw a line of people waiting and watching, anticipating their turn. Recently, a friend was passing through West University Place, a small city in the inner loop of our larger city, Houston, and they said, "What is Milk and Cookies? I drove by this place at 8:30 at night and saw this line of people around the block. Clearly, something was happening there!"

I responded, "Oh, it's amazing! But be careful, that place will change your life." Milk and Cookies is a little cookie and ice cream shop known for its amazing chocolate chip cookies, just down the street from Brent and Cassie's gym. They are life-changing cookies that are large and gooey and, well…just perfect. They are worthy of a long-line because they WILL change your life (and your waistline).

In Isaiah 44, something clearly is happening. The prophet Isaiah is proclaiming that when the Jews will be in captivity, God will raise up a deliverer. Isaiah 44:24-28 declares:

> Thus says the LORD, your Redeemer,
>   who formed you from the womb:
> "I am the LORD, who made all things,
>   who alone stretched out the heavens,
>   who spread out the earth by myself,
> who frustrates the signs of liars
>   and makes fools of diviners,
> who turns wise men back
>   and makes their knowledge foolish,
> who confirms the word of his servant
>   and fulfills the counsel of his messengers,
> who says of Jerusalem, 'She shall be inhabited,'
>   and of the cities of Judah, 'They shall be built,
>   and I will raise up their ruins';
> who says to the deep, 'Be dry;
>   I will dry up your rivers';
> who says of Cyrus, 'He is my shepherd,
>   and he shall fulfill all my purpose';
> saying of Jerusalem, 'She shall be built,'
>   and of the temple, 'Your foundation shall be laid.'"

What's so incredible about this text is that it proclaims hope to those who were irrelevant, exiled, and in bondage. This proclamation, made before Cyrus the Great was ever born, named him as a deliverer. It declared that something life-changing and extremely relevant was going to happen. These life-altering events took place in 539 and 538 B.C. respectively. The first significant action was the overthrow of the Babylonian empire by Cyrus, and his Medo-Persian army. Babylon falling to Cyrus represented a new day for the Jews in exile in Babylon. Cyrus was the one who proclaimed that the Jews could return to the city of Jerusalem and rebuild the temple in 538 B.C. Isaiah calls Cyrus God's shepherd, fulfilling His purpose, saying of Jerusalem,

"'She shall be built,' and of the temple, 'Your foundation shall be laid.'"

With that in mind, notice how the book of Ezra introduces us to this life-changing action as it opens with these words in Ezra 1:1-4:

In the first year of Cyrus king of Persia, that the word of the Lord by the mouth of Jeremiah might be fulfilled, the Lord stirred up the spirit of Cyrus king of Persia, so that he made a proclamation throughout all his kingdom and also put it in writing:

"Thus says Cyrus king of Persia: The Lord, the God of heaven, has given me all the kingdoms of the earth, and he has charged me to build him a house at Jerusalem, which is in Judah. Whoever is among you of all his people, may his God be with him, and let him go up to Jerusalem, which is in Judah, and rebuild the house of the Lord, the God of Israel—he is the God who is in Jerusalem. And let each survivor, in whatever place he sojourns, be assisted by the men of his place with silver and gold, with goods and with beasts, besides freewill offerings for the house of God that is in Jerusalem."

God was on the move to rebuild that which had been torn down. The Israelites had sought the welfare of the city of Babylon (Jeremiah 29:1-9) and now they were invited to the next step in the journey. The words of Jeremiah that proclaimed a hope and a future and a return to the land were upon them.

Take a moment and familiarize yourself with these words. Jeremiah 29:10-14 states:

"For thus says the Lord: When seventy years are completed for Babylon, I will visit you, and I will fulfill to you my promise and bring you back to this place. For I know the plans I have for you, declares the Lord, plans for welfare and not for evil, to give you a future and a hope. Then you will call upon me and come and pray to me, and I will hear you. You will seek me and find me, when you seek me with all your heart. I will be found by you, declares the Lord, and I will restore your fortunes and gather you from all the nations and all the places where I have driven you, declares the Lord, and I will bring you back to the place from which I sent you into exile.

Something was surely happening and about 50,000 Israelite lives were about to change.

CHAPTER 1

Fighting for Relevance: Understanding Your Fight Story

Let me introduce you to Decatur Wilson as he chronicles his fight story.

On January 16, 2013, my life came to a screeching halt. Everything I knew for certain became uncertain except my faith in God Almighty. My wife Cheryl discovered a lump on my back in late December 2012. A physician and a surgeon diagnosed it as a harmless fatty lipoma. It didn't need immediate attention but because the lump was the size of a tennis ball, I decided to remove it. What was supposed to be 45-minute outpatient procedure became two surgeries within 24 hours, which led to a Sarcoma cancer diagnosis. Sarcoma is a very rare cancer. The survival rate is very low.

After meeting with the oncologist in our home city of Charleston, SC and doing extensive research, we received a referral to M.D. Anderson Cancer Center in Houston. We knew no one in Houston. It was more than 1100 miles from our home. But God! God had gone before and prepared a way for my recovery in so many ways I could write a book on his grace, mercy, and provision at every turn. The doctors at M.D. Anderson advised me to begin treatment immediately! Cheryl and I flew back to Charleston and made plans for the six weeks of treatment.

Through Bible Study Fellowship my wife met the daughter of the late Karen Harrison who lived in West University Place near M.D. Anderson Cancer Center. As a matter of fact, Mrs. Harrison used to work at M.D. Anderson. Her mother had a ministry of allowing people who were in Houston for cancer treatment to stay with her in her home. Of course, we were not planning to stay with her. I am a general contractor and had full intentions of continuing to operate my company while in treatment. While Cheryl and I were driving back to Houston with a carload of office supplies to continue to work, we received two phone calls. The first was from Karen Harrison inviting us to stay in her home. The second was a realtor offering to purchase a property we did not have up for sale. They offered was to pay us twice the market price at that time. God was providing for our spiritual, physical, and financial needs. God knew our battle was going to last for 14 months with the first cancer. Fifteen months later, Cheryl was diagnosed with breast cancer. 18 months after that, I developed bladder cancer. Today, eight years later, we are residents of Houston, members at West University Baptist Church, and cancer free!

God provided family and friends in a strange place. We received the prayers, love, and friendship of a praying church family. God in His sovereign wisdom provided the financial and spiritual blessing we would need to sustain us through the illness. There are so many more instances where we have seen the Lord's hand at work during this fight, I could literally write a book on the goodness of the Lord through trials. Proverbs 19:21 tells us there are many plans in a man's heart but no matter what our plans are the Lord's purpose will prevail. We must trust in God's plan even when it does not align with our own.

WHERE DOES YOUR FIGHT STORY BEGIN?

For Zerubbabel and Joshua, it began when a new king came to town. They went from irrelevant to relevant, nearly over night. Cyrus the Great became the most powerful man on the face of the earth. Cyrus aligned the Persian tribes into a solid block of power thus defeating Astyages of Media after the Median troops deserted their king and defected to Cyrus. By conquering the Medes, conflict was certain with the Babylonians, as they and the Medes claimed much of the same territory.

After consolidating power in Asia Minor and overrunning the mountainous region between the Caspian Sea and the northwest corner of India, Cyrus set his eyes on Babylon. In 539 B.C. Cyrus defeated the Babylonians which proved to be a new day for many nations who had been captured by the Babylonians.

During an archeological excavation in Babylon between 1879 and 1882, the archeologist Hormuzd Rassam discovered what is now known today as the "Cyrus Cylinder." This cylinder was full of inscriptions that detailed Cyrus' policies. One of the most significant policies to the Jews was the policy for captured peoples to be permitted to return home and build sanctuaries to their own gods.[3] Warren Wiersbe states, "His policy with prisoners of war was opposite that of Babylon, for he encouraged the Jews to return to their land, rebuild their temple, and pray for his welfare. No doubt Cyrus extended this same privilege to other displaced nations and their gods." [4]

Zerubbabel, also called Sheshbazzar, was going to become Jerusalem's governor. He was in the royal line of David (1 Chronicles 3:17-19), and his fight story begins with this new opportunity to lead the charge to return to Jerusalem. This is true of Joshua, the High Priest at the time, as well.

Ezra, for whom the Old Testament book is named, entered the story by leading a second wave of Jews back to the Promise Land in 458 B.C. Ezra was a priest and a scribe. God used him to renew the word of the Lord in the lives of the people. Then, we are introduced to a man named Nehemiah, a cupbearer to the king. Nehemiah is an officer in the king's court. In 445 B.C., he is stirred to go back to Jerusalem and rebuild her walls.

YOUR FIGHT STORY

Knowing where your fight story begins is critical. It's here that something can be noted. There was a moment, a burden, a signpost, or a realization that altered the course of your life. Maybe it was a diagnosis, a call you received about your child from one of her teachers, a flood like Tropical Storm Harvey, or even the emergence of COVID-19. It only takes 20 seconds for your life to change!

Raymond shares one of his fight stories as he watched his wife Susan battle cancer. He states:

> In 2001, Susan was diagnosed with breast cancer. The cancer was very aggressive. She had to undergo both chemotherapy and radiation. I knew she would have to fight for her life to beat this disease. Susan would need all the support and love that I could give. The battle for me was to show strength for her to draw from during those times when she was very weak during her treatment. Susan would need to lean on me to help her over those bumps in the road. Suppressing those feelings of fear is difficult knowing there is a chance you may lose the love of your life. This is the time where your faith is tested and you raise your shield. We both questioned this situation and wondered why, but we kept our faith in our Lord who helped us. Susan was diagnosed a second time with a different kind of breast cancer in 2012 but it was caught very early. After surgery I'm

happy to say she is cancer free. We both have learned a lot since 2001. Today, we live our lives for the moments we have. We don't sweat the small things that may come our way. We know God is in control and that He loves us.

Notice how our fight stories begin with a sense that something just changed, or something must change. Our fight stories often entail what feels to be a vast climb or insurmountable odds. The tasks before us seem to be too great and we don't know where or how to begin. You know what I'm talking about, don't you? When you are weighed down by the moments before you and you aren't sure what to do next—that's when you have entered the ring and the fight is underway.

START WHERE YOU ARE WITH WHAT YOU HAVE

Not every fight is a fight for your life. Some stories, are filled with great opportunity. Some are calls for leaders to shift gears and make a difference. Some are sacrifices to become special as an athlete, a student, or a professional. Whatever they are, they are fights to stay relevant against the tide that is coming against you.

Zerubbabel, Joshua, Ezra, Nehemiah, along with those they lead, were stepping into the ring as the hammer was hitting the bell. New opportunities, experiences, even adversaries were about to emerge before them while they had to keep walking and keep fighting.

MY FIGHT STORY

In 2008, Dr. Barry Landrum approached me about his retirement. I had served alongside my pastor at West University Baptist and Crosspoint Church since 1997. I was his youth pastor and then became the associate pastor. We launched Crosspoint Church as our second campus in the city of Bellaire, another inner loop city in the heart of Houston, Texas, on the last Sunday of January of 2005.

As I look back, I realize we broke all the rules of multi-site ministry. We didn't have the same name on the church. We were only two miles apart. We took too many of the entrepreneurial types from our West University campus and sent them to the new location. Then, we didn't do video teaching. Instead, Barry handed me the bat and told me I was up. He and I would rotate pulpits, whether it was week to week or month to month.

Even as I write these words, I am humbled at the trust that he showed me. In February 2008, he told me he believed I was to be the next pastor of the church and that he wanted to know how I felt about that. As you can imagine, that was a tremendous moment for me, when my boss, mentor and friend in ministry extended that belief in me.

I prayed about it, discussed it with my wife Julee and told him I would submit to the process. We would see what the Lord had in store. In fall 2008, Barry announced his retirement date of May 2010. He highly encouraged the church to call me as their next pastor. Each Baptist congregation is self-governed, having the rights and responsibility to call her own pastor versus having one appointed by a bishop or other denominational structure. As a result, the church had the opportunity to make some adjustments to how it normally called a pastor. The church decided to put a team together to evaluate my capacity to move from the associate pastor role to senior pastor. If I didn't pass the test, or if there wasn't a sense of the Lord's leading, they would turn their search outward. We appreciated this opportunity and an evaluation process began.

In the meantime, Julee and I were doing our own evaluation. I wasn't sure this was God's will for our lives. Just as the church needed to hear from God and go through a good process, we needed to hear from God as we went through the process.

In March 2009, Julee had purchased tickets for a Chris Tomlin concert. She was nearly eight months pregnant with our daughter, Carson. Being months into this evaluation process, with both of us working and raising two boys, we knew that we just needed a night out together.

It was a great concert and a wonderful evening for just the two of us to be together. Toward the end of the performance, Chris Tomlin began to sing the song, "God of this City." The chorus declares:

> Greater things are yet to come,
> Greater things are still to be done in this city.
> Greater things are yet to come,
> Greater things are still to be done here.

As we listened and sang along, we looked at one another. We had just stepped into the ring. The bell was about to go off. At the very same moment, the Holy Spirit called us. The call became crystal clear—that my calling as pastor was to the city through the church. I thought God was to call me to the church, but this call surprised me. It was to the city, through the church. Tears began to emerge. We knew that God had spoken. We had to avail ourselves to this call.

TAKING INVENTORY

Naturally, my next question was, "What do I do next?" I had to start where I was with what I had. The first thing at my disposal was a willing people, as they extended a call to me and the intentional process of transition was truly underway. By God's grace, their willingness remains to this day. I have discovered that it is our people who are our greatest asset. Beyond that, I had some time: time to assess, time to plan, and time to learn. You see, Dr. Landrum, in his wisdom, prepared a year of transition for the church. This was a gift to me. He was willing to let me have some runway to prepare things beyond his leadership journey, while he finished well.

I also had somewhat of a plan. I looked at the next season as an opportunity to shape the staff in accordance with how we would need to function going forward. I saw ways we could honor Barry and Charlotte's leadership for their faithfulness over the previous 13 years. I also saw some gaps in my leadership capacity.

I also had the foundations of generosity that were being laid. We had just launched Casa El Buen Samaritano, a medical clinic setting out to serve the poor in three zip codes. Most of the clients of the clinic are Spanish speakers. They are uninsured and live 150% below the poverty line. Casa had a board of doctors, leaders with vision and limitless opportunities to share the good news with the people of our city.

Beyond Casa, we had the beginnings of what we today call Mercy House Ministries. Mercy House began through the burden of Beverly Metzger. Beverly is a nurse at M.D. Anderson Cancer Center. She had lived in one of the northern suburbs of the city but moved into the city after she was widowed. Beverly purchased a nice town home just a few blocks from the medical center. One of her prayers was that she never wanted to be alone.

Beverly's compassion, along with her nursing skills, led her to begin to invite some of her patients to stay with her. Many patients who come to M.D. Anderson have a stage three or four diagnosis and are sent here from around the United States. Some even come from other countries to receive the care at M.D. Anderson that they can't receive at home. As you can imagine, the expense of traveling to a new city as well as finding a place to stay near the medical center can be physically, emotionally, and financially overwhelming. Beverly heard stories from some of her patients and naturally began to invite them to stay with her while they were in town for their medical treatment.

All the while, I would meet people, nearly every Sunday, in our worship services who had just come to the city for medical care. I would pray with them and try to encourage them while I had them there, but I found myself wishing we could do more.

As you start where you are, let me ask you a question: What is unique to you? What relationship, proximity, burden, ability, strength, or skill, do you have at your disposal? Start there and build on that. In both the story of the clinic and Mercy House, which has now expanded to three permanent locations, our proximity to the Texas Medical Center and the emerging spirit of generosity was our uniqueness.

WHAT DO YOU WANT?

As you start where you are, with what you have, make sure you include a list of what you want but don't yet have. The biggest thing I wanted and didn't have was the ability to disciple the church regarding finances. I had always admired the way that Barry led the church financially. He was an executive. He could dig into the numbers and raise money. He was gifted at teaching on stewardship. I didn't have any experience leading in this manner. I saw a gap in my leadership and decided I needed to learn a new skill. I went on a journey, connected with Patrick Johnson and Dan Hall of Generous Church, then hired Dan to be my coach. That relationship has changed my life in countless ways.

In the course of my work, I occasionally have the privilege of pouring into leaders who move from the second chair into the first. That's my story. I'm glad to share what I can with emerging first chair leaders. In a recent conversation, one of these leaders emailed a financial presentation to me and asked me to analyze it.

After 20 minutes, I asked him if we could get on a call. I called him by name and said, "This is a good presentation. It's solid. It's factual. It's accurate. It tells the story. And it looks like it's put together by your business administrator." I proceeded to ask him, "Where is the vision of where you are going? What do you want to see happen? This has to be in here as well."

They were living in the land of deficit. They hadn't given raises in three years. They were stuck financially. He had just started his second round of this fight to which God had called him.

Those questions helped him to see, not just what was there, but what was missing. They also stirred him to ask, "What do I want the outcome to be?" Have you taken the time to ask yourself, "What do I want the outcome of this fight to be?" Trust me, you won't always get what you want, but having a clear picture of what victory looks like is vital for the fight you are waging.

A clear victory might be a declaration of being cancer free. A clear victory might be a great comeback story for your congregation. It might be your son or daughter off drugs and once again walking with the Lord. What is the clear victory? What is it you want?

GOD'S PROVISION FOR YOUR FIGHT

As we talk about our fight stories and watch the story of Ezra and Nehemiah unfold, look for God's abundant provision. See how at every turn, there was always enough. Watch God provide over and over. Watch Him move mountains. See Him go before you. Be humbled by His hand! This happens as the book of Ezra opens, as Nehemiah goes before the king, and as you and I step into the fight. There are people, resources, connections, breakthroughs, God-sized challenges, and outcomes that will be a part of your story. You have a generous God who is generous with his love, support, resource, and wisdom. He is so generous that He did not spare His only Son, but gave Him up for us. He is so generous that He stands in the fiery furnace with you. He is so generous that He fights your battles for you. He has such provision that He knows how to take the cup from you or give you the grace to endure it. His word in Proverbs 2 says that, "…He holds wisdom in store for the upright." God has a store house of wisdom just for you. He is such a generous God, and in your fight, you are going to need all the ways that He provides as you go round after round after round, fighting for yourself, fighting for your children, fighting for your marriage, fighting for your name, or fighting for his kingdom. As you fight, believe He is right there in the fight with you, going before you and fighting for you at every turn.

Dan Hall, my long-time coach, mentor, friend, and the one God has used to train me in understanding God's abundant kingdom, often says, "Provision is simply God being pro the vision he has already given you." Zerubbabel, Joshua, Ezra, and Nehemiah all saw this truth take place in their fight stories and if you keep your eyes open to it, you will as well.

THE FOUNDATION OF YOUR FIGHT STORY

Inherent in the words above is a foundation of faith in the God of the Bible. You may not yet possess this faith, or you may be brand new to faith. I can encourage you to see God's generosity because His gospel announces to us that He is a giving God. John 3:16 begins, "For God so loved the world that He gave..." God's fight story for us entails His compassionate love for us that moved the Father to give the Son as a sacrifice of atonement for our sin. Jesus, the Son of God, went willingly to the cross on our behalf. He willingly gave Himself up for us. He stood in our place. He took on our sin and shame, and it is by His stripes that we are healed, forgiven, and set free.

Jesus then rose from the grave and offers to us life, everlasting, abundant, and free. His resurrection from the grave secures your resurrection from the grave as well. God's fight story entails defeating sin, death, evil, and suffering. It's the ultimate fight story, and the wounds in his hands and feet proclaim that God saw you to be worthy of that fight.

If you have never taken Jesus to be your Savior and Champion, I would encourage you to consider this good news – that your sin, which separates you from God, can be removed by placing your faith in the work that Jesus did on your behalf on the cross. When you trust Jesus, you are no longer a slave to sin, but you are free in Him. When you take Jesus, you are saved, sealed by the Holy Spirit, and are called a child of God.

Would you like to lay a foundation of faith by receiving Christ as your Savior right now?

It's a simple prayer that you can pray right here. Pray it aloud and from the heart.

Lord Jesus, I believe you are the Son of God and I admit that I am a sinner in need of a Savior. I believe you died for me and rose again from the dead. I ask that you come into my life to save me today. I place my faith in you. Thank you for fighting for me and giving me this foundation of faith to build upon.

Now, as a Christian, you are invited into a wonderful journey called walking by faith. You are called to live by faith and to hold fast to the things of God found in His word. When you take Christ as your Savior, you move from wondering about life and wandering through life, to certainty and purpose. His fight for you is the best deal going.

REFLECTION QUESTIONS:

1. Have you taken Christ as your Savior? If so, write out God's fight story for you and how you came to faith in Jesus. This is the foundation of your fight story.

2. What's your fight story and when did it begin? It may have been something negative like a job loss, enduring abuse, or a diagnosis. It could be a burden to make a difference that God placed on you. When did it begin and what are you learning as a result?

3. What changed? What seems insurmountable? What about this fight was or is overwhelming to you?

4. What does a clear victory look like to you? What is it you want? Write out in a sentence what your clear victory looks like.

5. How has God already provided for you? Chronicle the ways you have seen him speak, provide, move mountains, make provision, or open doors for you.

CHAPTER 2

Fighting for Your Future: Being Wrecked by a Burden

In spring 2004, Dr. Barry Landrum, the pastor of West University Baptist Church, was approached by a man in our church named Royce. Royce was a contractor. He built homes, subdivisions, and commercial buildings. Royce also was on the board of a little Christian school named Bellaire Christian Academy that met at the First Baptist Church of Bellaire.

As happens in churches, First Baptist Church Bellaire had gone through some very trying times. Their pastor at the time believed if they sold their building, they could get a new start somewhere else with a different model of ministry. Royce wasn't excited about this prospect, but he was just a member of the school's board, not a member of the church. In many ways, his ability to influence the situation was very limited.

But Royce couldn't shake the sense from the Lord that he was to do something about it. He couldn't rid himself of the need to find a way to keep that location in the heart of the city as a light house for God. It was prime real estate. He could ultimately develop the four and a half acres into houses, and he would have made a tremendous amount of money. But he felt compelled to buy it, then offer it to our church at his cost. Royce wanted our church to reach more people for the gospel of Jesus Christ at that location.

I remember the day when Barry came to me and said, "Royce just put a price on a church. He wants to know if we want a shot at it." I am sure I said something like, "Let's go for it!" Royce and Sylvia leveraged everything they owned as collateral and closed on that property. Dr. Landrum put together a team and a process to search out whether our congregation should have a second location just two miles away.

Now, keep in mind, when Dr. Landrum came to West University Baptist Church in 1996, the church was coming out of a difficult season. We had one service running about 350 people. Now, less than ten years later, we had two services and a sense of great renewal happening with a church running around 600 – 700 people. This was a great comeback story in itself. But did we have the faith and resources to buy and launch a new campus less than two miles away? Would the people really want to go? Would the others support it? Could we pull this off?

Those were the questions swirling around in our hearts. What I have noticed on my own journey is that it's the questions of new beginnings and significant change that keep us from fighting for our futures. But God knew where to start—with a builder. You see, what Royce saw wasn't a problem but an opportunity. He could see beyond the moment where the gym building was to be torn down because of a termite infestation in the support structure. He could see beyond the poor condition of the carpet, paint and furniture. He could see beyond the messy middle of the process of committee work and congregational approval.

He and Sylvia could see a location in the inner loop of the fourth largest city in the United States, filled with people, alongside our original campus, also filled with people. He's a builder -- and builders don't just see what is. They also see what could be.

BURDENS LEAD TO VISION

When you look at each of the main characters of the stories of Ezra and Nehemiah, you see that their fight began with a burden which led to a vision. From the world's most powerful man to a cupbearer to the king, God uses people who can see more than what is before them to mobilize others to join the adventure.

Notice the burden and gift of vision in the opening words of both Ezra and Nehemiah.

> In the first year of Cyrus king of Persia, that the word of the Lord by the mouth of Jeremiah might be fulfilled, the Lord stirred up the spirit of Cyrus king of Persia, so that he made a proclamation throughout all his kingdom and also put it in writing:

> "Thus says Cyrus king of Persia: The Lord, the God of heaven, has given me all the kingdoms of the earth, and he has charged me to build him a house at Jerusalem, which is in Judah. Whoever is among you of all his people, may his God be with him, and let him go up to Jerusalem, which is in Judah, and rebuild the house of the Lord, the God of Israel—he is the God who is in Jerusalem. And let each survivor, in whatever place he sojourns, be assisted by the men of his place with silver and gold, with goods and with beasts, besides freewill offerings for the house of God that is in Jerusalem."

The Lord was ahead of all the parties involved to accomplish His plan. Notice it says, "…the Lord stirred up the spirit of Cyrus king of Persia…" This is so amazing to me! God works through kings, nations, and governments to fulfill what He has already declared. He had declared through Jeremiah that after 70 years of captivity, the Jews would return to Jerusalem to rebuild the temple and her walls. God was stirring Cyrus' spirit to fulfill what He had already promised.

Second, Cyrus was charged to build a house for God. Keep in mind, this is the most powerful man in the world ruling the largest kingdom on earth. Verse 2 states, "Thus says Cyrus king of Persia: The Lord, the God of heaven, has given me all the kingdoms of the earth, and he has charged me to build him a house at Jerusalem, which is in Judah." Is Cyrus an outlier, or might we too need a vision larger than ourselves? You see, if he, the most powerful man in the world was stirred to build God's house, then who can claim exemption from this task?

Third, to build this house, Cyrus invites the Jews to return to Jerusalem and empowers them to rebuild the temple. This task of rebuilding the house of the Lord is just too great for any one man to do alone. But Cyrus could make sure the provision was made by taxing the people, by inviting them to make freewill contributions, and by making a contribution himself.

Ezra 1:3-11 states:

> "Whoever is among you of all his people, may his God be with him, and let him go up to Jerusalem, which is in Judah, and rebuild the house of the Lord, the God of Israel—he is the God who is in Jerusalem. And let each survivor, in whatever place he sojourns, be assisted by the men of his place with silver and gold, with goods and with beasts, besides freewill offerings for the house of God that is in Jerusalem."

> Then rose up the heads of the fathers' houses of Judah and Benjamin, and the priests and the Levites, everyone whose spirit God had stirred to go up to rebuild the house of the Lord that is in Jerusalem. And all who were about them aided them with vessels of silver, with gold, with goods, with beasts, and with costly wares, besides all that was freely offered. Cyrus the king also brought out the vessels of the house of the Lord that Nebuchadnezzar

had carried away from Jerusalem and placed in the house of his gods. Cyrus king of Persia brought these out in the charge of Mithredath the treasurer, who counted them out to Sheshbazzar the prince of Judah. And this was the number of them: 30 basins of gold, 1,000 basins of silver, 29 censers, 30 bowls of gold, 410 bowls of silver, and 1,000 other vessels; all the vessels of gold and of silver were 5,400. All these did Sheshbazzar bring up, when the exiles were brought up from Babylonia to Jerusalem.

As this king and leader begins to move other people to this great task, notice these first words. Maybe you assume they were just what kings say, but maybe the stirring in Cyrus is so profound, he can't help but speak a blessing. He says, "…may his God be with him…" Normally, the subject is saying to the sovereign, "Long live the king!" or, "God save the king!" But here, the sovereign is saying to the subject, "May God be with you!"

How would your burden and vision for your future change if you were absolutely certain that the God of the universe, the maker of heaven and earth, was with you? Would it change how you fight? Clearly, the author of Ezra is trying to show off the sovereignty of God to even rule over kings of foreign nations. Yes, the 70-year captivity has been a long challenge for the Jews. But God was moving, stirring and providing. He was making His presence in the situation known.

Even the king's movement was used by God to stir other leaders. The heads of the households of the tribes of Judah and Benjamin, as well as the Levites and priests are stirred. Verse five says, "⁵ Then rose up the heads of the fathers' houses of Judah and Benjamin, and the priests and the Levites, everyone whose spirit God had stirred to go up to rebuild the house of the Lord that is in Jerusalem." Leaders don't just move followers. They move other leaders. Burdened leaders who take action cause other leaders to ask questions -- "Am I supposed to get involved with this? Am I to gather my family and move?" This creates space for God to move in the lives of these leaders and many others who join the journey.

I saw this happen through a barbecue fundraiser for one of our pastor's granddaughters. Ronny and Ruth Barner faithfully served West University Baptist Church for more than 52 years. He was the worship pastor and administrator for 38 years. After he retired, he served in a part-time capacity as the senior adult pastor. He is now Pastor Emeritus. Ronny's granddaughter became ill and needed some specialized treatment that was only available at a medical center in the country of Panama. She could not walk. The goal was to do very expensive therapy to enable her to possibly walk again.

My wife, Julee, came to me one day and said, "I feel moved to do something for Ronny and Ruth and their family. They have done so much for this church for so many years and I am sure we can do something for them." She then said, "I think we need to do a barbecue fundraiser after church one day."

Like the great leader that I am, I said, "Honey, we can't do a fundraiser for this. If we do a fundraiser for them, we set precedent and will have to do a cake walk, carwash and lemonade stand for any and everybody that asks." She simply said, "I don't care about all of that. The Barners have given their lives to this church and we need to do something."

Well guess what began to happen? That's right, I went to the office and got the ball rolling. We began to invite people to the barbecue fundraiser and made people aware of the significant need of over $100,000 for the four-part treatment plan. Now, I'm not sure what kind of barbecue fundraiser raises over $100,000, but we were going to take a swing at it. I could see in my wife's eyes and her heart that the amount of money wasn't the issue. It was the effort that counted.

As the event got closer, I received a call from one of our members: "My wife and I would like to give a sum of money for this need. We want to remain anonymous, but also want to challenge you to see if you can get it matched." I told him that I would like to attempt to get it matched then I would get back to him on the results of that challenge.

I got after it and began working the phones. I talked to a number of our leaders. They all chipped in for this need. Pretty quickly, the gift was doubled. Meanwhile, I was waiting to hear back from a gentleman who led a team that oversaw a charitable fund. He told me this type of need was exactly why that fund was created so many years ago, and they too matched the gift. I was so blown away by this exchange that I called my wife and the original family making the donation. I said, "We haven't just doubled the gift, it has been tripled."

The day before the fundraiser I got a call from a family who wanted to contribute to this need. In that call, I got to tell the story of what was unfolding and how the gift had been tripled. By the time we got off the phone, this family decided to match the initial gift. Before we ever served a plate of barbecue we had already raised the resources.

How many times have we thwarted the plans of God by saying, "We can't do that! It will set a precedent?" How many times have we shut down the hearts of burdened people who feel compelled to put up a fight on behalf of another because of policy or procedure? Oh, that we would have the heart of God to be stirred and moved to meet needs! I still remember the day when Ronny and Ruth's granddaughter got up out of her wheelchair and walked. She was restored. We too were moved because this preacher's wife wouldn't take no for an answer.

Leaders move leaders with their burdens. The heads of households in the tribes of Judah and Benjamin, the two tribes that made up the southern kingdom of Judah, along with the priests and Levites, were so moved by God, they in turn moved their families. They had planted gardens. They had married and sought to increase in Babylon. Many Jews stayed right where they were. But God was doing something new. This attracted nearly 50,000 others to join them on the journey, moving toward a brighter future.

SAME SONG, SECOND VERSE

In this same story, burden leads to vision a second time. But this time, it's not the king who decides to build. This time, it's one of the king's officers, his cupbearer named Nehemiah. Ninety years have passed. It's now 445 B.C. Warren Wiersbe says, "In 457 there had been a small revival under Ezra, but now it was 445, and God was looking for someone to go to the ruined city and restore safety and order. Nehemiah was to be that person."[5] To move Nehemiah, God had to weigh him down with a burden. Notice this burden in Nehemiah 1:1-4.

> The words of Nehemiah the son of Hacaliah.
>
> Now it happened in the month of Chislev, in the twentieth year, as I was in Susa the citadel, that Hanani, one of my brothers, came with certain men from Judah. And I asked them concerning the Jews who escaped, who had survived the exile, and concerning Jerusalem. And they said to me, "The remnant there in the province who had survived the exile is in great trouble and shame. The wall of Jerusalem is broken down, and its gates are destroyed by fire."
>
> As soon as I heard these words I sat down and wept and mourned for days, and I continued fasting and praying before the God of heaven.

FIGHTING FOR SOMETHING GREATER THAN OURSELVES

Do you hear the fight forming in Nehemiah's heart? These fights come to us as burdens. They wreck our lives. When God is about to move in a family, in a church, or in a city, He often brings a collision full of burdens and lays them right at our feet. God says, "Hey, I want you to do something about this mess." That's what happened to Nehemiah, and I am convinced that's what happened to Royce and Sylvia. They became so burdened that all they could do was fight for that corner property at 4601 Bellaire Boulevard. They didn't want another buyer to turn it into retail space or homes. They didn't want the fire department to move its headquarters there. They wanted a gospel witness established there for many years to come. They were weighed down for the glory of God to remain in the house of the Lord.

Have you ever been weighed down like this? Have you ever been overwhelmed by a need so big that you don't know even where to begin? What do you do when you get weighed down like this?

Define Reality

Leaders define reality. They don't shy away from it. They don't run from it. They face it. Here was Nehemiah's reality:

- Devout Jews prayed for the peace of Jerusalem. As you see Nehemiah's prayer in Nehemiah 1, you see he loved God and revered his word. Thus, Nehemiah would be familiar with the Psalms of Ascent and the commendation of Psalm 122 to pray for the peace of Jerusalem. But how could one pray for a city's peace if the walls were torn down? Notice Psalm 122 which states:

I was glad when they said to me,
    "Let us go to the house of the Lord!"
Our feet have been standing
    within your gates, O Jerusalem!
Jerusalem—built as a city
    that is bound firmly together,
to which the tribes go up,
    the tribes of the Lord,
as was decreed for Israel,
    to give thanks to the name of the Lord.
There thrones for judgment were set,
    the thrones of the house of David.
Pray for the peace of Jerusalem!
    "May they be secure who love you!
Peace be within your walls
    and security within your towers!"
For my brothers and companions' sake
    I will say, "Peace be within you!"
For the sake of the house of the Lord our God,
    I will seek your good.

Nehemiah had been born in Babylon and had never been to Jerusalem, so everything known to him about Jerusalem was second-hand. But that didn't mean it wasn't accurate information. Though the temple has been rebuilt by this time, the walls still lay in ruin. Jerusalem is still being mocked and taunted by her neighbors.

Psalm 79:1-4 says of Jerusalem:

> O God, the nations have come into your inheritance;
>   they have defiled your holy temple;
>   they have laid Jerusalem in ruins.
> They have given the bodies of your servants
>   to the birds of the heavens for food,
>   the flesh of your faithful to the beasts of the earth.
> They have poured out their blood like water
>   all around Jerusalem,
>   and there was no one to bury them.
> We have become a taunt to our neighbors,
>   mocked and derided by those around us.

- To get to Jerusalem, it would take four months to travel the nine-hundred-mile journey. This wasn't an easy journey, as there were many criminals along the way.

- I'm sure there was an uncertainty of the reception he would receive in Jerusalem if he just showed up telling the people that he was going to try and fix their problem.

- The thought of getting the king's permission to leave seemed crazy. He was trusted with the king's wine. As the cupbearer to the king, Nehemiah faithfully put his life on the line every time the king wanted wine. He tasted it first to ensure it was not poisoned. Releasing Nehemiah to this task was a great risk for the king, and Nehemiah knew this as well.

- Add to this the sense that he felt responsible for the sins of a previous generations, and you see that Nehemiah is in a difficult place.

- Could he really leave the comforts of Babylon? Babylon was the most advanced city in the known world. As Alan Platt says, "He would be exchanging the palace for the desert wilderness and his bed for hard ground." [6]

All of this was probably swirling around in Nehemiah's mind. What swirls around, often binds us up. The angst is almost palpable as Nehemiah is driven to his knees with weeping. Defining reality can do this to us when we are wrecked by God-sized burdens.

So, what's your reality? What burdens you? What's at the root? How do you get a clear picture of what journey lies before you?

Prayer and Fasting

The second thing we see Nehemiah do as he is wrecked with this burden for the people and walls of Jerusalem is enter into a season of prayer. As you read various stories in the Scriptures, you realize that prayer is simply talking to God. It appears that Nehemiah prayed for approximately four months. He was initially burdened in the month of Chislev (December) and didn't make his request before King Artaxerxes until Nisan (April). We only have one recorded prayer, but notice the context. Nehemiah didn't just pray one time, but repeatedly. Notice these clues in Nehemiah 1:4.

> As soon as I heard these words I sat down and wept and mourned for days, and I continued fasting and praying before the God of heaven.

Nehemiah heard these words about the remnant of people and the walls. He was wrecked by them. So, he hit his knees and set aside time to process this pain. He wept and mourned for days. Then, he continued fasting and praying.

What are we to conclude about Nehemiah's time in mourning? First, he refrained from eating. Many times, in the Scripture fasting is a component of time set aside for mourning. When you fast, you intentionally set something aside for the sake of something greater. People fast from all sorts of things – food, alcohol, social media, television. Fasting is a way to stay focused so that you can prioritize, pray, dream, or think.

Second, he used this time to pray. Nehemiah simply talked to God and shared his pain with Him. Do you pray? Do you take time in your day and throughout your day to talk to your Heavenly Father? Hebrews 4:14-16 instructs us. It says:

> Since then we have a great high priest who has passed through the heavens, Jesus, the Son of God, let us hold fast our confession. For we do not have a high priest who is unable to sympathize with our weaknesses, but one who in every respect has been tempted as we are, yet without sin. Let us then with confidence draw near to the throne of grace, that we may receive mercy and find grace to help in time of need.

Third, he may have used this time to search the Scriptures to have a better understanding of why Jerusalem, the city of God's choosing, was still a dangerous, devastating place. Nehemiah used this time of mourning to look for answers and gain understanding.

HOW NEHEMIAH'S PRAYER INFORMS OURS

Have you ever prayed for something so far out of your control and for such a long time that you ached deep in your soul? I'll never forget an exchange with one of our members who told me, "You have never really learned to pray until your children leave your home." Her statement came during our own prayer journey for our oldest son. He had gone off to college and had gotten a rough start. There were a lot of factors in play, and though he was seeking to be honorable, this challenge couldn't be fixed overnight. Every day as our son would be getting out of bed on the east coast, we would be on our knees praying for that day. We would beg God for peace. We would ask God to intervene. We would pray for favor on our child. We kept him before our Lord repeatedly. We ached in the depths of our soul for something beyond our control.

I've watched several parents through the years do this very thing. Their fight becomes something of real significance happening in the life of their son or daughter. It drives them to their knees. They pray and plead and continue to be steadfast and unmoved, pleading with God for a breakthrough. As I write these words today, I know a number of families praying for God to intervene as only He can. I have watched them take this posture for many months now and I find myself seeking to encourage them in the fight. I'll say to them, "Keep fighting. Keep showing up. Keep up the fight."

Nehemiah records a prayer in the opening verses of Nehemiah chapter 1 that help us. How did he pray? What did he say to God that helps us know how to pray for the burdens that have wrecked us?

Let me categorize his prayer and then ask you to note it when you read it. Nehemiah's prayer entailed:

- Praise
- Intercession
- Confession
- Petition
- Personal Request

Look at Nehemiah 1:5-11 and note where you see each of these elements of Nehemiah's prayer.

> And I said, "O Lord God of heaven, the great and awesome God who keeps covenant and steadfast love with those who love him and keep his commandments, let your ear be attentive and your eyes open, to hear the prayer of your servant that I now pray before you day and night for the people of Israel your servants, confessing the sins of the people of Israel, which we have sinned against you. Even I and my father's house have sinned. We have acted very corruptly against you and have not kept the commandments, the statutes, and the rules that you commanded your servant Moses. Remember the word that you commanded your servant Moses, saying, 'If you are unfaithful, I will scatter

you among the peoples, but if you return to me and keep my commandments and do them, though your outcasts are in the uttermost parts of heaven, from there I will gather them and bring them to the place that I have chosen, to make my name dwell there.' They are your servants and your people, whom you have redeemed by your great power and by your strong hand. O Lord, let your ear be attentive to the prayer of your servant, and to the prayer of your servants who delight to fear your name, and give success to your servant today, and grant him mercy in the sight of this man."

Now I was cupbearer to the king.

Praise

Do you see how Nehemiah opens with praise? In verse five he extols the Lord, the God of heaven. The use of this term Lord was a "…reminder of God's rule and (that his) authority rests ultimately upon his creation and ownership of all things and people." [7] The term "God of heaven" alongside Lord, reminds us of Psalm 24:1-2 which proclaims:

> The earth is the Lord's and the fullness thereof,
>   the world and those who dwell therein,
> for he has founded it upon the seas
>   and established it upon the rivers.

Nehemiah is proclaiming that all that exists belongs to his God. All that is and ever will be is subject to the Lord God of heaven. He then declares of God that He is great and awesome. In other words, He is too vast to comprehend, and He is to be feared, honored, and revered. I believe that this is why, even after the season of mourning, that during that four-month season of prayer where he "prayed…day and night," Nehemiah continued to fast. This didn't mean that he didn't eat for four months. Maybe he only ate one meal a day. Or maybe he fasted a few times a week. But the point is that Nehemiah uses prayer and fasting to show God his humble position as he praises Him for his greatness.

In his praise of the Lord, Nehemiah proclaims that He is a covenant keeping God. This is the basis of what we see Nehemiah pray in verses seven through nine. It also harkens back to Exodus 34 where the Lord passes before Moses and proclaims his name. This portion is foundational in understanding that our God is a God of covenant promise. Exodus 34:6-7 states:

> The Lord passed before him and proclaimed, "The Lord, the Lord, a God merciful and gracious, slow to anger, and abounding in steadfast love and faithfulness, keeping steadfast love for thousands, forgiving iniquity and transgression and sin, but who will by no means clear the guilty, visiting the iniquity of the fathers on the children and the children's children, to the third and the fourth generation."

To be one of steadfast love is to be one full of loyal love and faithfulness to a covenant. Nehemiah knew this of God. He knew that the Lord had established a covenant with Abraham and his descendants. He gave him a land and a nation. This covenant with Abraham was an unconditional covenant.

Nehemiah also knew that the Lord had given Israel the Law of Moses, a conditional covenant of blessing or curses based upon their obedience to Him. Studying Deuteronomy 28-32 is foundational to understanding the rest of the Old Testament. It's foundational to understanding Israel's captivity by Babylon in the first place. If they were an obedient people, they would prosper in the land and their enemies would be subdued. If they were disobedient to the covenant, they would endure the curses of the covenant – the very reason why Nehemiah was born in Babylon, and not in Judah.

But what you and I must understand is that in Jesus, we are under a new covenant—a covenant of salvation, growth, and glory that has come to those who take Christ as Savior. He is the Lord God of Heaven. His covenant is no longer a covenant written on stone, but it is written on our hearts. It's not limited to the Jew only, but also to all the nations. It's not based on our work, but on the work that

He did for us on the cross and when we pray to the Father through Jesus the Son, as we are stirred by the Spirit, we should begin with praise. Because all things are held together by the Lord Jesus Christ. They were made by him and for him. Colossians 1:15-20 declares:

> He is the image of the invisible God, the firstborn of all creation. For by him all things were created, in heaven and on earth, visible and invisible, whether thrones or dominions or rulers or authorities—all things were created through him and for him.
> And he is before all things, and in him all things hold together. And he is the head of the body, the church. He is the beginning, the firstborn from the dead, that in everything he might be preeminent. For in him all the fullness of God was pleased to dwell, and through him to reconcile to himself all things, whether on earth or in heaven, making peace by the blood of his cross.

For whom or what are you fighting? Go to your knees and praise Jesus that He is the one, the Lord God of Heaven, who is holding all things together. He is the one to exalt today as you fight for yourself, your family, your city, and your church. Begin with praise.

Intercession

I have two dogs named Bella and Stella. They are golden doodles. Bella is big at about 75 pounds. Stella is smaller at about 25 pounds. They are a hoot when they wrestle. Bella and Stella love ice. It's their treat. It's the most economical treat on the market. There is an unlimited supply and it costs me nothing to provide it to them.

But I don't hand it out to them unless they ask for it. Our icemaker is near the coffee pot. When they hear me making coffee in the mornings, or when I'm standing near the coffee pot in our kitchen, they come asking for ice. They must have some sort of agreement worked out between them, because Stella is the first one to get an ice cube, no matter what. Then, she stands near the front shoulder of Bella and waits for her to drop her first ice cube. It's as if Bella asks for an extra one for her buddy when she is given one. She does this by consistently dropping the first one given to her and doing nothing to pick it up. Instead, Stella is right there to scoop it up, and then trot off to eat her two cubes of ice.

Interceding is asking on behalf of another. Nehemiah's four-month season of prayer was to make intercession for the people of God who resided in the dangerous city of God. He would pray for them repeatedly. The first part of verse six says, "…let your ear be attentive and your eyes open, to hear the prayer of your servant that I now pray before you day and night for the people of Israel your servants…" He can't help but pray for them. He can't help but ask God to help them. He can't help but make a plan for them.

Confession

The rest of verse six and then verse seven says, "…confessing the sins of the people of Israel, which we have sinned against you. Even I and my father's house have sinned. 7 We have acted very corruptly against you and have not kept the commandments, the statutes, and the rules that you commanded your servant Moses."

Nehemiah is getting down to business now. As he prays, he comes to God admitting his sin and the sins of his nation. His admission that, "We have acted very corruptly against you and have not kept the commandments, the statutes, and the rules that you commanded your servant Moses," is his agreement with God's just sentence upon the Jews for placing them into captivity. Deuteronomy 28:36-37 pre-scribes just one of the things that will happen to the nation of Israel if she does not keep the covenant. It says:

> "The Lord will bring you and your king whom you set over you to a nation that neither you nor your fathers have known. And there you shall serve other gods of wood and stone. And you shall become a horror, a proverb, and a byword among all the peoples where the Lord will lead you away."

If Nehemiah never requested passage to Jerusalem and the opportunity to rebuild the walls, he was right to confess Israel's sins. Because as you continue to read in Deuteronomy, you see God's promise to restore when a heart of repentance is established. Deuteronomy 30:1-3 declares:

> "And when all these things come upon you, the blessing and the curse, which I have set before you, and you call them to mind among all the nations where the Lord your God has driven you, and return to the Lord your God, you and your children, and obey his voice in all that I command you today, with all your heart and with all your soul, then the Lord your God will restore your fortunes and have mercy on you, and he will gather you again from all the peoples where the Lord your God has scattered you."

Repentance precedes restoration. Nehemiah is repenting for his sins and the sins of the nation asking God to be merciful.

Is there anything for which you need to repent? I find that there usually is. But maybe the fight that has made its way to your front doorstep is there to get your attention. Maybe it's there to cause you to pick your head up and ask God to search your heart and life. Clearly, he was doing this with his people.

Petition

Notice how Nehemiah moves immediately to petition. His request is simply for God to do what He had already promised to do if the nation repented. In essence, Nehemiah says, "God, I've found it. I see in the law here that You said that You would restore us if we repented. So, God, I'm leading the charge. Do what You said You would do." Here he quotes Deuteronomy 30:2-3 that we just read. I can just imagine as he sees God's heart as revealed in the law and the promise to restore the nation, he becomes excited and expectant. He asks God to listen to his prayer and to others who pray in this same way, because he is believing that something significant is about to happen.

Personal Requests

As Nehemiah's prayer comes to a close, he simply asks for favor. He asks that the covenant keeping God of heaven would put a grace into the heart of his boss because he was about to ask him for a lot. He prays for success and that the king would be merciful. Nehemiah 1:11b says, "…and give success to your servant today, and grant him mercy in the sight of this man." To receive mercy is to have something you deserve withheld from you. Even this request is full of the knowledge that the king could kill Nehemiah for even bothering him with this request. Nehemiah has a depressed disposition when he appears before the king, and no one was to enter the king's presence downcast. Nehemiah's plea for mercy was a plea for his life. He knew he had an appointment to serve the king, but he also knew that he couldn't change his disposition.

Beyond the plea for mercy was the plea for success. Nehemiah needed what the king had. He needed provision, protection, and passage to attempt what he was feeling led to do. In this one relationship was all those things and Nehemiah knew it.

Nehemiah wept, fasted, prayed and planned. He had a burden that wrecked him, but he had a faith that guided him. Now, it's go time.

REFLECTION QUESTIONS

1. Have you taken the time to define reality? Here are the questions I asked you just a few minutes ago. Take a few minutes to define the landscape of your burden.

   • What's your reality?
   • What burdens you?
   • What's at the root?
   • How do you get a clear picture of what journey lies before you?

2. Have you taken the fight to your knees? As you are burdened for something beyond your control, ask God to give you vision that:

   a. He is in control
   b. He will lead you
   c. He will provide for you
   d. He is up to something that will bring him glory.

3. Will you take a season to fast and pray for that which overwhelms you? How often will you fast and from what will you fast? (I have found that its best with something of significance like a meal, and then grow the discipline from there. Consider one time per week skipping lunch or dinner and then set aside time to pray, journal, dream, and plan).

4. Of all the Scriptures listed in this chapter, which one spoke to you the most? What do you think God is saying to you through it?

5. How does God want to use this battle you are in to grow you as a person of prayer? Circle the type of prayer(s) that you want to grow in:

    - Praise
    - Intercession
    - Confession
    - Petition
    - Personal Request

6. Write out a prayer(s) that focuses on the type of prayer you just circled.

CHAPTER 3

Fighting for Sustainability: You Can't Give Out What You Don't Have

Each of us has struggles. Some are external – known and seen by everyone. Others are internal and get exposed in times of trouble. Sonya shares her fight story about the loss of her father soon after her first child was born. She says:

> Life seemed to change instantly when I got a phone call that my dad was rushed to hospital. He had a stroke which led to a brain aneurysm. Eight days later, as we stood faithfully by his side, continually praying for a miracle, God chose to take him home to be with Him. As a brand-new, postpartum mom of a one-and-a-half-month-old, the feeling of true joy had taken a

dramatic turn in the opposite direction. I felt a loss I had never known.

I had always had the mentality of an overcomer. Truth be told, it ran in my family. My grandfather taught it to us. He modeled living with my grandmother who had bipolar disorder for as long as my mom could remember. I didn't seem to know any other way to deal with the loss of my dad but to push through. For a while, my sweet little Emma kept me going. Of course, I was a believer and knew that the Lord was there, but I had a lot of anger. Questions arose like: "Why would God do this to me and our family?!" or "Why now?" Yet I choose to suppress my feelings which led to heightened anxiety and depression in the years to come.

Wonderful people around me encouraged me to take the next step toward counseling and medication. I am so thankful for these people. A common misunderstanding in our "church" mentality tells us you can pray your way through. And yes, God is big enough and can save at ANY point. I began to learn that God wasn't ignoring me or refusing to rescue me. This was my journey. This was to be my story – one to share. As a ministry wife, I often kept my pain hidden. Even when many people would want to come and ask me to pray for them. It was hard to turn the table, look them in the eye, and let them know I was hurting.

When Pastor Roger asked, "What does a clear victory look like to you?" I realized that it is a victory to know I am broken and in need of Jesus daily. I don't have enough on my own. Although the pain still is with me, either in the grief of my loss almost 18 years ago, or my ongoing battle with anxiety and depression, I am still learning about keeping my dependency on Him. 2 Corinthians 12:9, speaks truth in my life: "My grace is sufficient for you, for my power is made perfect in weakness."

I am so thankful for Sonya's transparency in sharing her internal fight. One of my biggest struggles, for as long as I can remember, has been my weight. It's been a battle. As a kid, I was heavy. I was fit as a high school and college student. But then, when I got married, I began to put weight on. I gained the typical ten pounds a year and before I knew it, I was pushing 300 pounds. I am tall, so that has worked in my favor, but that simply masked to some what was obvious to me. Even in seasons where I would have success with my weight by losing 15 or 20 pounds, I would inevitably get stressed, gain the weight back, and put on a few more pounds. Do you know this struggle? It's been one of my fights throughout.

Your weight may not be your battle. You may battle mental health issues like depression or anxiety. You may battle insecurity and the need of acceptance. You may battle chemical dependency or have some other struggle. Getting help when we need it is vital.

The battle rope experience in the gym showed me that the path I was on was not sustainable. I wasn't taking care of my health. I wasn't tending to my soul. I was just striving to serve others because that is what I was supposed to do. I wasn't taking care of myself. I didn't take a sabbath. I didn't fast. I didn't consider my food choices, and I thought that just by working out a few times a week, I would be fine. But I began to fall asleep on the couch when I sat down to watch a TV show. I didn't have the energy I wanted. I was grieving the loss of my best friend in ministry from our staff. I was grieving my coach's tragic accident that left him paralyzed from the neck down. This injury took place when he came to Houston to serve me, our team, and our church body in a crisis. I was grieving that those two men were stripped away from me in a five-day period.

Beyond the grief, I realized I had isolated myself and wasn't engaging with the staff or the church body as I should have. Waking up to the realization that I was empty – exhausted physically, spiritually, emotionally, and socially – was critical to my ability to keep walking. I had to make a change if I was going to stay in the fight. I was at a place where I realized that I had nothing left to give and it scared me.

How can we be sure we have what we need to fight? How can we build sustainability into our lives so we can get stronger as the adversity gets heavier? My friend, Dr. Jeff Frey, who has his doctorate in not-for-profit leader health and flourishing says we must, "…pursue self-care for self-sacrifice." When we take on a burden or fight, we must recognize how vital it is for us to sustain ourselves so we can endure the fight and continue well beyond.

This seems to be intuitive for Nehemiah going into this battle as he goes before the king. Nehemiah knows exactly what he needs if he is going to be successful and if the project is going to be sustainable. Nehemiah 2:7-9 states:

> I also said to him, "If it pleases the king, may I have letters to the governors of Trans-Euphrates, so that they will provide me safe-conduct until I arrive in Judah? And may I have a letter to Asaph, keeper of the royal park, so he will give me timber to make beams for the gates of the citadel by the temple and for the city wall and for the residence I will occupy?" And because the gracious hand of my God was on me, the king granted my requests. So I went to the governors of Trans-Euphrates and gave them the king's letters. The king had also sent army officers and cavalry with me.

When Nehemiah went before the king, he sought sustainable provisions. He sought the timber that would be necessary to rebuild the city gates (There were ten gates, so this was a lot of timber). He sought safe passage through challenging territories. He sought what was necessary to get him to Jerusalem and get the work done. He started with the end in mind and knew what he would need day in and day out to finish the project well.

All too often, the challenge of the moment and the burden of the season may cause us not to see the end. We launch out to engage in the fight and we are empowered to go through it. Our prayer life is renewed, our dependency on our Lord is like no other time in our life, and we see God work wonders. We are fed daily by His Word. We are held by His hand.

We are lifted repeatedly. We wage the war and even see victory, yet the fight requires so much from us that we neglect taking care of ourselves. We get to the other side, and we crumble. The fight has demanded so much that when we get to the other side, we want to quit. If that's you, you are not alone. I understand that exhaustion physically, emotionally, spiritually, and relationally. Before we move ahead, we must understand that we have to take responsibility for our lives beyond the fight we are in.

I didn't see it coming. I didn't know the toll the loss of two great men, in a five-day period, would have on my life. As a result, I was ready to crumble. I was depressed. I was broken. I was faking being okay. I was ready to quit the ministry and go and do anything else. But on the other side of it, I can see now that this is not uncommon.

Elijah the prophet experienced this sense of depression to the point of crumbling. He spoke the word of God boldly. He took on the wicked King Ahaz and his wife Jezebel. He told the king that at his word, it would not rain, and it didn't rain for three years. Elijah was in hiding all this time. He was fed by ravens. Later he was fed by a widow whose provisions would be miraculously replenished each day.

Elijah called for a final fight on the mountain top. He defeated the prophets of Baal at Mt. Carmel. He was all in. But after the fight was over and after experiencing an amazing victory, Elijah crumbled. He fell prey to the fear of Jezebel who issued a death sentence and began to hunt him. With nothing left in the tank, he ran. He fell headlong into depression and despair, and it nearly killed him. As you fight for yourself, I want to encourage you to fight physically, spiritually, and emotionally, and for your relationships. Fight for yourself because you can't give out what you don't have.

THE FIGHT AGAINST DEPRESSION AND DESPAIR

I have asked Dr. Ryan Rush, the founder of Empowered Homes, and the pastor of Kingsland Baptist Church, if I can share this next section with you. Ryan wrote this portion on depression and Elijah, and it's so good, I have used it at least a half dozen times in various settings. He had his own battle with depression, as I did as well. It's not uncommon for those in a fight, as depression is America's number one emotional disorder, and it's not just for "weak people." Elijah was one of the most amazing, bold leaders in the Scripture!

There is a difference between ordinary sadness, which we all experience from time to time, and out and out depression. Elijah wasn't just sad, he was depressed. What is the difference? Dr. Aaron T. Beck says, "Depression differs from sadness and anxiety differs from worry in that they are more intense, last longer, and they significantly interfere with effective day-to-day functioning." Psychologists have described depression this way:

"A feeling of helplessness and hopelessness that leads to intense sadness."

While depression is the primary focus, anxiety is also in view here. Clinical Anxiety is obviously distinct from clinical depression, with different markers – such as uncontrollable, racing thoughts, and avoidance of situations. One psychologist noted that often those with clinical anxiety are, "…deeply afraid that something bad is going to happen or that they might lose control of themselves."

Interestingly, anxiety might be considered the other side of the coin of depression. Let me share just a few facts with you:

- Roughly 50% of people diagnosed with depression will also be diagnosed with an anxiety disorder. [8]

- Both conditions are associated with low amounts of serotonin and dopamine in the brain. It can be helpful to think of anxiety and depression as two versions of the same thing.

- Depression and anxiety have become so pervasive in our society that it is now called, "…the common cold of mental illness."

- Approximately 40 million Americans 18 or older suffer from anxiety disorder, 17 million adults suffer from major depressive disorder, and 10 million are severely depressed.

- An estimated 3.2 million adolescents aged 12 to 17 in the United States had at least one major depressive episode last year.

- Further, depression and anxiety don't care how old you are. They can impact anyone.

Once a person falls into depression and anxiety, the danger is that it often degenerates into darker and darker phases, which can lead to not only a lost quality of life, but even tragedy. While this is not the most enjoyable subject, we've got to talk about it. For many of you, this IS your fight. Or, it's the fight you see your loved one wage every single day.

Before we go any further, I want to say just a few simple things:

1. If you are depressed or anxious, you are not alone in your plight.

Years ago, there was a young midwestern lawyer who suffered such deep depression that his friends kept knives and razor blades away from him for fear that he might harm himself. This man wrote:

"I am now the most miserable man living. If what I feel were equally distributed to the whole human family, there would not be one cheerful face on earth. To remain as I am is impossible. I must die or be better."

The man who wrote those words was none other than Abraham Lincoln. Winston Churchill, perhaps the greatest Prime Minister in the history of Great Britain, the man who was famous for saying, "Never give up, never, never, never, never give up," called depression a "black dog" that followed him all his life.

Often Christians find it hard to admit when they are depressed because they feel depression is a sign of ungodliness. They feel they are not close to the Lord as they should be. In fact, many people mistakenly think that the Bible teaches that depression is a sin, and that Christians should never be depressed. But nothing could be further from the truth. Some of the greatest people in the Bible battled with depression. Moses, the greatest leader Israel has ever known, the man who single-handedly delivered the people of Israel from Egyptian bondage, once became so depressed that he said in Numbers 11:15, "If you will treat me like this, kill me at once, if I find favor in your sight, that I may not see my wretchedness." Jonah, the prophet who was swallowed by a great fish, and lived to talk about it, expressed the same desire in Jonah 4:3, "Therefore now, O Lord, please take my life from me, for it is better for me to die than to live."

In light of this, consider Elijah. Elijah was a mess. He withdrew from normal activities. He was isolated. He was gloomy. He felt hopeless and helpless. He was not eating well. He was extremely irritable. Practically all of us have experienced at least a few of these emotions at one time or another. Why do we get depressed? How do we end up with anxiety?

What many people don't understand is you can't just snap out of depression and anxiety. It can feel overwhelming when you're walking through it. The Mayo Clinic describes depression as sometimes literally feeling like your arms and legs are heavy. Every person I've ever spoken with who's walked through this has had the feeling like they are carrying a heavy weight around. As Ryan Rush says, "It's a matter of life or death! But Jesus came that we might have life."

2. **If you're depressed or anxious, I want you to know there's hope for you today!**

Jennifer's fight story is so helpful here. God doesn't always work in the same way in every case, so continue your journey of treatment until you know that you have been set free. But I want you to notice how she fought to overcome obsessive compulsive disorder and see the hope that exudes her life today.

Back in the fall of 2005, around the time Hurricane Rita was to make landfall, I noticed an urge to double, triple, or even quadruple, check things. For example, after cooking in my apartment I would turn off the stove even though I knew I had turned it off, I felt I still needed to double and triple check it. My fear was that the stove was still on and soon my apartment would catch on fire. This carried over to checking to see if I had locked my apartment door or doubting if I had shredded everything I was supposed to at work. Did I turn off the light switch? Did I lock my car door? All of these doubts crept up on me. I began to fear I had said the wrong thing while talking to a friend at work. I developed intrusive thoughts. These were thoughts I didn't want to have. These thoughts were telling me I needed to go back and check things and go back and review conversations. I doubted so many things. This caused me to feel incredibly anxious. I allowed these doubts and thoughts to control me. It was an awful way to live. I knew that this was not the way God had intended for me to live my life. It was a very sad time. It seemed that nobody around me had doubts. No one else seemed to struggle like I did.

I saw a clinical psychologist and was diagnosed with Obsessive Compulsive Disorder, or OCD. Anxiety in and of itself is a huge umbrella that takes on many different types of forms. One of anxiety's forms is OCD. Therapy helped me, but I still struggled a great deal. It was incredibly hard work. I prayed and asked God to take the OCD away from me. I worked hard with my therapist, but I still struggled with OCD. In January 2011, our first son was born. It was a very happy time in my life, but I was still struggling with OCD. I had a very supportive husband, mother, and father. They all wanted me to get better. My husband really had to practice tough love, which is what I really needed. With OCD, you're given an obsession. That obsession causes tremendous anxiety and fear. I shed a lot of tears. I wished that the OCD could be taken away from me. I was so tired of allowing anxiety to control me. I knew I was better than all of it. I felt so guilty and ashamed of living in a world full of doubt. I felt like I had let my husband and my children down because I just couldn't get a grip on my OCD.

In fall of 2013, I experienced a breakthrough. I attended Denise Glenn's Bible study, "Freedom for Mothers." Denise happened to be the one teaching her own study. I was due to have our second son in November. I remember confiding in friends at that time letting them know about my OCD, explaining to them that I knew that my grandmother had suffered with anxiety while she was on earth. I distinctly remember somebody telling me that just because my grandmother suffered from anxiety that didn't mean that I had too as well. I didn't have to continue the family trend and continue carrying the anxiety "torch."

I had previously cried out to God for years asking Him to please take the OCD away from me. To please heal me from it. I've been a believer in Jesus since I was in the second grade, but God really got a hold of me in this Bible study. The study taught me that Jesus, when He was on the cross, had already taken care of all my anxiety and OCD. Every nail that pierced his skin was my anxiety and my OCD. He already paid for everything for me. I could surrender everything to Him. My anxiety and OCD could truly be left at the foot of the cross. I imagined walking across the stage at our church to a tall wooden cross. I imagined taking my OCD to the foot of the cross, where it belonged. With this mindset I began to feel a perfect peace from the Lord. I realized I was finished living a life where I allowed anxiety and OCD to control me. I was free to live for Jesus – no longer bound by any chains. I could turn the stove off the first time and walk away.

Since coming to this amazing realization in 2013 I was able to share my testimony with our Mother's of Preschoolers group at our church. I now talk about it so freely and have been able to encourage another family member who is also struggling with OCD.

I praise God for Who He is and what He did for me and not only me but for all of His children. It's so humbling to know that He loved all of us enough to take away our anxieties, doubts, and fears because He wants us to have a full life completely dependent on Him and not controlled by anxieties. I'm thankful that God has allowed me to have OCD. I still have some slip ups from time to time, but I'm trusting in Jesus and casting ALL my anxieties on Him. Having OCD has allowed me to tell my story and to help encourage others that suffer through similar anxieties.

I'm thankful for Jennifer's fight story and how she is living with hope. Let's spend a few minutes understanding Elijah's symptoms.

Physical Exhaustion

Notice 1 Kings 19:1-5.

> Ahab told Jezebel all that Elijah had done, and how he had killed all the prophets with the sword. Then Jezebel sent a messenger to Elijah, saying, "So may the gods do to me and more also, if I do not make your life as the life of one of them by this time tomorrow." Then he was afraid, and he arose and ran for his life and came to Beersheba, which belongs to Judah, and left his servant there.

> But he himself went a day's journey into the wilderness and came and sat down under a broom tree. And he asked that he might die, saying, "It is enough; now, O Lord, take away my life, for I am no better than my fathers." And he lay down and slept under a broom tree. And behold, an angel touched him and said to him, "Arise and eat."

The first thing we notice is Elijah's physical exhaustion. Exhaustion or some physiological challenge can lead to this extra weight and feeling of being overwhelmed. Elijah seems to be worn out, but your depression or anxiety may be a physiological issue that runs deeper than hunger or fatigue. Don't neglect that.

Depression is seldom something that is "all in your head." In Elijah's case, he was physically worn out. He had been fasting for a long time, so his body was weakened. He had just finished a run of marathon proportions. Elijah ran a full day into the wilderness without stopping. His strength was gone. He was hungry. He was thirsty. He was physically exhausted. On top of that, he was under a threat for his life. Ryan Rush says:

> You can mark this down: When your body is physically rundown and worn out; when your diet and nutrition is bad and unhealthy; when you are not getting enough rest; when your nerves are jangling from pressure and anxiety; you are an easy prey, a prime target for the monster of depression.

Emotional Pain

In verses two and three we see spiritual and emotional letdown set in. It says:

> Then Jezebel sent a messenger to Elijah, saying, "So may the gods do to me and more also, if I do not make your life as the life of one of them by this time tomorrow." Then he was afraid, and he arose and ran for his life…

Do you see how heavy this is? His physical exhaustion leads to spiritual and emotional challenges as well. It's like a new level of heaviness as the mind and the feelings go hand in hand. Remember, Elijah is already physically exhausted. Now he's not thinking straight about the situation.

Everybody, from time to time, struggles with their emotions. In fact, people who claim they have no problem controlling their emotions, sometimes have the greatest problems with pent up feelings that need to be let out. Those emotions can wreak havoc on your personal prayer life and your walk with the Lord if you don't address issues.

Depression or anxiety don't always happen due to a "trigger event." But they may be magnified because of upsetting circumstances. Maybe we have heard about the sudden death of a loved one, a job loss, or a diagnosis—some sort of heartbreak. Something causes emotions to come crashing down, even after soaring sky high.

You know when things go wrong, or when things don't go exactly like we think they ought to, we might feel like curling up in a fetal position and talking about how bad things are, and how unfair life is. It's a natural spiral. Even though depression isn't necessarily related to our sin, it can lead to disconnecting from the very help we need from the Lord.

Social Isolation

Notice the third challenge we see in Elijah. 1 Kings 19:3b-4 states:

> …and came to Beersheba, which belongs to Judah, and left his servant there. But he himself went a day's journey into the wilderness…

Even worse than physical exhaustion and emotional and spiritual unrest, Elijah is now facing all of this alone. That's when the weight is overwhelmingly heavy. Life is very dark for him. He left his companion behind. We'll read more in a moment, but when Elijah does have a conversation with the Lord in verse ten, he says four terrible words. You might not have said them, but you've likely felt them: I alone am left.

So now Elijah is spiraling. He's physically spent. He's emotionally turned upside down and he is all alone. In fact, he feels abandoned. He has no one who could relate to his challenges. So where does that leave him?

...(he) came and sat down under a broom tree. And he asked that he might die, saying, "It is enough; now, O Lord, take away my life, for I am no better than my fathers." And he lay down and slept under a broom tree.

Have you been there? What are the answers? Does God care for us when we don't know how to fight anymore? When we have given all we can, have no fight left, feel abandoned and all alone, what are we to do?

The reason I love this passage is that we get to watch Elijah's Creator treat his depression. Look at the sequence and look at the solutions.

1 Kings 19:5b-8 says:

And behold, an angel touched him and said to him, "Arise and eat."

And he looked, and behold, there was at his head a cake baked on hot stones and a jar of water. And he ate and drank and lay down again. And the angel of the Lord came again a second time and touched him and said, "Arise and eat, for the journey is too great for you." And he arose and ate and drank, and went in the strength of that food forty days and forty nights to Horeb, the mount of God.

Physical Restoration

How does the Lord treat Elijah's depression? The first thing we see is physical restoration. I love that God began here. He made a physical provision for Elijah. As soon as Elijah had prayed to die, God did two things for him. First, he put him asleep and then he gave him something to eat. Rush says:

"Now that is both precious and priceless. Elijah wanted to die, but God gave him a nap. Then God baked him some "angel food cake." Then He gave him something to drink. Then He gave him some more rest."

What you may need right now is an earlier bedtime and a balanced diet. God is the Great Physician. He knows more about health than anyone. God understands that you need to have good nutrition. You need to have a reasonable amount of rest. For many people, a part of this physical renewal is medical help.

We need to do the same thing with mental health. Don't let anybody tell you to suck it up if you're dealing with this stuff. It's real. It's physiological.

I love that before God dug any deeper, he addressed the physical. What might you fight for regarding your physical life? Karen Lamb said, "A year from now you may wish you had started today."

Spiritual and Emotional Restoration

1 Kings 19:9-11a states:

> There he came to a cave and lodged in it. And behold, the word of the Lord came to him, and he said to him, "What are you doing here, Elijah?" He said, "I have been very jealous for the Lord, the God of hosts. For the people of Israel have forsaken your covenant, thrown down your altars, and killed your prophets with the sword, and I, even I only, am left, and they seek my life, to take it away." And he said, "Go out and stand on the mount before the Lord."

What happens next is fascinating. If you recall the story, you will remember that there is a strong wind, but it is evident that it is not the Lord. Then, there is an earthquake, but again, it is not the Lord. Then there is a fire, but this also is not the Lord. Finally, there is a small whisper. That was God. It was here that Elijah got alone and quiet with the Lord and poured out his soul. You see, after physical restoration, we are in desperate need of spiritual and emotional restoration. Now after Elijah was rested and refreshed, he was then ready to do business with God. God had healed him physically. Now God was ready to touch him emotionally. What God did for him; God can do for you. You've got to learn to spiritually rest.

Again, this doesn't mean that the reason you're depressed is because you've rejected God, or that He has rejected you. That's not it at all. I'm saying that when you're in the midst of the darkness of this, you can get your beliefs about how He sees you all out of whack. You need to saturate yourself with truth from God's Word.

Turn off the TV, the phone, the radio, and the computer for an hour and get alone with God. Let Him speak to you. Saturate yourself in Psalm 121:1-2, which says,

> I lift up my eyes to the hills.
> From where does my help come?
> My help comes from the Lord,
> who made heaven and earth.

Get into the Word of God. Claim the promises of God. When you are being afflicted with depression, remember Psalm 34:19 which says,

> Many are the afflictions of the righteous,
> but the Lord delivers him out of them all.

Social Restoration

Let's look at what happens next. 1 Kings 19:15-18 states:

> And the Lord said to him, "Go, return on your way to the wilderness of Damascus. And when you arrive, you shall anoint Hazael to be king over Syria. And Jehu the son of Nimshi you shall anoint to be king over Israel, and Elisha the son of Shaphat of Abel-meholah you shall anoint to be prophet in your place. And the one who escapes from the sword of Haz-

ael shall Jehu put to death, and the one who escapes from the sword of Jehu shall Elisha put to death. Yet I will leave seven thousand in Israel, all the knees that have not bowed to Baal, and every mouth that has not kissed him."

Remember earlier when Elijah complained that God had left him all alone? Right here God tells him there are 7,000 who are loyal to the Lord! He's not alone; he just needs to take his eyes off himself. After the physical restoration and the spiritual retreat, the Lord calls us to social restoration. If you want to get on a path to wellness, you're going to need authentic community, as you were created for connection. When you do not have it, you will suffer.

Martin Luther was correct when he said:

"Isolation is poison for the depressed person. For through this the Devil attempts to keep him in his power."

Somebody put it this way: "Don't give in - get out." It might not necessarily be a meeting with someone for that purpose. It might be connecting with someone to help them or to go with them to help someone else. Someone once asked Carl Menninger, the famous psychiatrist, "What would you advise a person to do who is experiencing deep depression and unhappiness?" Many expected him to reply, "Go see a psychiatrist." But to their amazement he said:

"Lock the door behind you, go across the street, find somebody that's in need, and do something to help them."

There's a sequence to God's solution for Elijah. You could think of it as a cycle: Address the physical needs, the spiritual needs, and the social needs. Then go back regularly and address the physical needs, the spiritual needs, and the social needs. Don't ever assume you've reached a point of invincibility where you can neglect any of the three. But here's the good news: when you address these things, there is hope to get well. You don't have to keep carrying that weight around!

HOW 90 DAYS CAN CHANGE YOUR LIFE?

What do you need to sustain the fight? What do you want to see happen physically, spiritually, emotionally, or relationally in your life? What action do you need to take in order to avoid crumbling after the fight is over?

There are several tools online for an assessment of how you are doing at any moment in time. Dr. Jeff Frey offers an assessment that will give you a snapshot picture of ten areas of your life.[9] The result will be a pie graph of your sense of fulfillment in areas such as your:

- Finances
- Relationships
- Physical Well Being
- Emotional Health
- Professional Fulfillment
- Spiritual Growth
- Intellectual Stimulation
- Environmental Enjoyment
- Organizational Discipline
- Recreational Fulfillment

What I have found to be so compelling in using this tool is that it shows me where I am fulfilled and moving right along, and where I am lacking fulfillment. It clarifies for me where I can act and see progress. I have also found if I move in one area of my life, it will create traction to bring other areas where I need work into alignment.

You may not need an assessment to know where you want to grow, improve, or act. You have been answering questions along the way. You already know it's time to get going. But action needs a destination. Your journey needs a path to take. So, how do you get from where you are to where you want to go?

I have found that 90-day periods of time are significant segments to create movement and momentum in my life. They are short enough to keep a goal before me and long enough to see real progress. I use Michael

Hyatt's Full Focus Planner to help me build a plan and execute it. This planner is broken into the quarter system and allows me to see each week as an opportunity to make progress toward my big goals. At the beginning of each quarter, I write out where I want to be 90 days later and what strategy I will use to get there. I used these tools to help me lose 50 pounds and to keep my weight off.

REFLECTION QUESTIONS:

1. In previous seasons and previous fights, did you ever crumble after the fight? If so, can you pinpoint why you crumbled?

2. What do you want to see change in your life over the next 90 days? Do you want better physical or mental health, spiritual growth, improved relationships? Write out a clear goal for this area that starts with the words, "90 Days from today, I will … "

3. How would you describe the state of your mental health? Have you ever been depressed or battled anxiety? What ways are you battling for your mental and emotional health?

4. What does it look like for you to pursue self-care in order to live a life of self-sacrifice?

5. What systems do you have in place to assist you to build sustainability for your health, spiritual growth, and emotional and mental health?

SECTION 2

Fighting for Your Home: Navigating the Messy Middle

A grandmother fought on her knees for her grandchildren and their spouses. Notice the principle she deploys as she knows exactly for whom she is fighting. This grandmother writes:

> One fall, one of my granddaughters in her late 20's was visiting me and shared her heart's desire to be married and have a family. She had high standards as a Christian with a good job and her own home. We earnestly asked God to find a good husband for her. I felt a strong urging to stop begging God to give her a husband but rather to begin praising and thanking God for the man He was going to send to her. I shared this with her. We pledged to continue with that mindset and just thank Him for what He would do.

Within two months a young man she knew from work as well as her church approached her. Even though he knew she had been encouraging him to date one of her friends, he wanted to date her. Within one year they were married.

Subsequently, a brother of hers was eager to find a soul mate and had tried all types of dating including on-line searches. But he never pursued any of the ladies he dated more than a couple of dates. I again suggested to the granddaughter that we start praising and thanking God for the woman He would send to this young man who would be the right companion for him. She committed to do that with me. She also said she was going to share this with her brother.

Within approximately two months, a godly young woman expressed an interested in the young man to his sister. He called to ask her for a date immediately. They have been seeing each other ever since. Marriage is not on the horizon yet, but we believe God worked.

Ironically, the other brother who is in the military, unmarried, and not very involved in church due to his travel overseas, was also interested in finding a wife. After one of his overseas assignments, he called me and said he was going to start looking for a church. He visited several places and finally settled on a church. In the church he became acquainted with a beautiful Christian woman who is a nurse but who has also been on many mission trips. They are engaged and will be married next Spring.

Most stories begin at the beginning. That's sort of obvious -- at least it was when I was a kid. As my kids came along, they would say, "Oh, Star Wars? That's Episode 4. They went back and made Episodes one through three since that came out." To this day, I still don't know the whole story, or at least the order of the story. In Star Wars fashion, I want to advance Nehemiah's story about two-thirds of the way through. The temple is rebuilt but the walls of Jerusalem still lie in ruin. Nehemiah, the cupbearer to the Medo-Persian

King, Darius, has been given permission to return to the land of his fathers to rebuild the walls. The king has even made provision for his journey.

As Nehemiah arrives and surveys the land, he gives a great speech to motivate the people to begin to build. They start the work on the gates and the walls. The chronicler records a great spirit of teamwork that came to the people. They entered the messy middle, where the task is harder, and the work takes longer than anyone anticipates. You may never have rebuilt a wall, but if you are raising kids, you know the struggle I am talking about. The people of Jerusalem encounter resistance from within and from without.

As Nehemiah assesses the landscape, he decides it's time for another speech. In Nehemiah 4:10-14 we see this exhortation:

> In Judah it was said, "The strength of those who bear the burdens is failing. There is too much rubble. By ourselves we will not be able to rebuild the wall." And our enemies said, "They will not know or see till we come among them and kill them and stop the work." At that time the Jews who lived near them came from all directions and said to us ten times, "You must return to us." So in the lowest parts of the space behind the wall, in open places, I stationed the people by their clans, with their swords, their spears, and their bows. And I looked and arose and said to the nobles and to the officials and to the rest of the people, "Do not be afraid of them. Remember the Lord, who is great and awesome, and fight for your brothers, your sons, your daughters, your wives, and your homes."

This is one of my favorite sections in this story, just like Star Wars is my favorite movie of all the episodes. This is the hinge moment when things are about to go north or south. This is that time in the crucible where we are going to find out what Nehemiah and the people on the
wall are made of. Like a lot of our lives today, we pick up this book and find ourselves already in the middle of a fight.

THE MESSY MIDDLE IS WHERE LIFE REALLY HAPPENS

In some ways every day is the messy middle at home. If you live alone, it's as messy or ordered as you want it to be. If you are a newlywed, nothing seems messy. Well at least until conflict begins because he is messy, and you aren't. Navigating how to live together becomes a bit of a mess.

When your children arrive, everything is new. With the oldest, it's a lot of firsts—the first bath, first crawl, first steps, first to play little league, go to middle school, high school, graduate and then head to college. But when kids two, three and four come around, it's just a mess.

The messy middle is where life really happens. It's where our greatest character is formed. It's where we learn to overcome challenges and embrace opportunities. It's where we learn to resolve conflict or not. It's where we will press ahead or where we learn to quit. It's Luke, Han and Leia getting caught in that trash compactor and never giving up. Imagine if they had just given up right there. We would only have half of one episode.

The messy middle moments make history. How we react when the adversity is at its greatest determines the outcome of our life's walk. As Nehemiah assesses the situation he sees the discouragement of his labor force, the adversity from those who would intimidate them, and the admonishments of the Jews who didn't live in Jerusalem. Nehemiah decides it's time to double down.

His challenge to them in verse 14 says, "And I looked and arose and said to the nobles and to the officials and to the rest of the people, "Do not be afraid of them. Remember the Lord, who is great and awesome, and fight for your brothers, your sons, your daughters, your wives, and your homes."

WHAT IS YOUR GREATEST FEAR FOR YOUR HOME?

Have you stopped to answer that question? What is your greatest fear at home? Is it:

- Divorce?
- Children addicted to drugs?
- Your kids walking away from the faith?
- Some sort of tragedy occurring?
- A terminal illness?

The truth is, there are so many fears that can hold us back and take us captive. Those who were set against the Jews rebuilding were making significant problems for them. They had intimidated the Jews living outside the city. They were calling them to come away from this project and salvage their lives.

In the messy middle when fears rise up, we must also rise up and stand on the foundation of our faith. In these moments, we need to heed Nehemiah's words as he assesses the situation and says, "Hey team, your God is greater than your biggest problem or fears. Let's not let up." Because God is great and awesome, we don't have to be afraid of anything that comes against us. Instead, we can fight for our families with all that we have.

I was with one of our dear senior adults recently as he was placed on hospice care. Paul and Willene have meant a lot to our church and to me for many years. As Paul and I were talking, I said to him, "Paul, I want what you've got. When I am old and dying, I want to lay here satisfied just like you are. I want my children and their children and their children to be walking with the Lord, just like yours are. What a legacy!" Tears came to both of our eyes as he said, "Amen." There was a deep satisfaction in him as we reflected on four generations walking with Jesus with many serving on the mission field for many years.

Their story might have been different if Paul and Willene's children hadn't seen them battle through the messy middle of raising three kids. How different would their legacy be if instead of multi-generational faithfulness, there was multi-generational abandonment or drunkenness? That's the fight we are in, and the fight Nehemiah knew they were facing. Nehemiah knew that if they let up in this messy middle, where chaos and fear-filled rhetoric reigned, these walls would not be built in his lifetime and their actions in that moment would impact generations to come.

That's the humble realization I have come to when challenging husbands and wives in their marriage struggles. Sometimes the moments are so raw and difficult that I have to say to them, "The actions you take in the next two weeks will set the course for your children's view of marriage and your grandchildren's view of marriage for their lifetime! Your actions today have a 30-to-50-year runway. Will you give them a legacy of faithfulness, or will they have to adjust to two Christmases, two birthday parties, and the awkward experience of not having their parents sit on the same row at their wedding?"

Now, before I go any further, please know that I am not picking on you if you have walked the road of divorce. That's not my intent. I know that every story is different. I am not trying to heap shame or condemnation upon you. Please forgive me if that is how I have made you feel.

Instead, I am trying to reach the reader who is pondering this way out, as the middle has gotten a lot messier than they ever believed it could. I want us to stop where we are today and play these scenarios out in our minds before we ever get to them. I want us to envision our children's pain when we must tell them the news, and I want it to keep us from taking that path. I want us to see the hurt on our spouse's face when we must share with them the news of our unfaithfulness. I want us to envision the ache, pain, and devastation we will cause when we decide to give up the fight. When we give up the fight, that's when bondage sets in. That's the exercise we need to do in our mind's eye to help us from doing it in real life.

KNOWING WHO YOU ARE FIGHTING FOR

Knowing who you are fighting for drives your fight. Nehemiah names who he wants them to fight for. He says, "…and fight for your brothers, your sons, your daughters, your wives, and your homes." His admonition to them is to stand up, not just for yourselves, but for your brother and his family, your marriage and your spouse's well-being, your children, and their futures as well.

Even if you are a single adult hoping for a family, your actions today should be taken considering the family God will give you tomorrow. I was counseling a college student who made some bad decisions and was struggling to find his way. His emotions were high. His struggle was real. The conflict with his parents was driving a wedge in their relationship. I could have confronted him on these things, but instead, I challenged him to do the right things that he knew to do—to honor his parents, to put Christ first, and to set the things of the world aside. I told him, "I want you to understand that the decisions you are making right now inform your future far more than you know. I want you to see a brighter future because you learn to walk with God. I want you to see yourself standing before God, your friends and family, and to see your bride coming down the aisle. I want to be there to tie the knot for you. Make choices today in light of the bright future you long for tomorrow." I asked him to envision playing golf or going fishing with his dad while he brought his son along. Knowing who you are fighting for is huge. How you carry yourself and the decisions you make today will prepare your tomorrow. Fight well. Fight with righteous standards. Fight because your God is great and awesome!

REFLECTION QUESTIONS:

1. Describe in a sentence or two what the messy middle of your life looks like in this season of life?

2. Has there been a time in the past where you realized that the moment you were in was the hinge moment where you had a decision to make? It may have been a messy middle struggle related to your work or your marriage or something with your children. As you look back, are you glad for the decision you made, or do you wish you had a do over? Explain why you answered the way you did.

3. What is your greatest fear at home? Is there a moment of failure that you should proactively envision so as to avoid the pain and devastation of that moment at all cost?

4. When you are lying on your death bed and hospice has been called in to make you as comfortable as possible, what do you want your legacy to be?

5. How might your prayers change because of reading this grandmother's fight story?

CHAPTER 4

Fighting for Your Marriage: Cultivating Marital Bliss

If you have been married for any length of time, you probably have a fight story that involves your marriage. Denise shares how God's power resurrected her marriage.

I found myself fighting with my husband only a few days after I had promised to "love and cherish 'til death parted us." How did that happen? We were both strong believers from wonderful Christian homes. Our parents' marriages had lasted for decades. We thought being madly in love and being Christians would mean it would be peaceful sailing in our marriage. Wrong! We quickly discovered we were two strong-willed people with Type A personalities. We were in a power struggle from the beginning of our marriage. That struggle lasted for seven miserable years.

On our seventh wedding anniversary, I announced to David that I was leaving him. I knew it was wrong. I knew it would hurt our families and our church. But at that moment, it was the only thing I knew to stop the pain. My shocked and hurt husband decided not to accept my resignation. Instead, he decided we were going to fight for our marriage and led us in prayer on our knees beside our bed. That night, broken before God, we cried out to Him a one-word prayer: Help!

God heard our cry. A few days later, some godly women in our church invited me to a prayer meeting that changed our lives. When I shared that our marriage was in shambles, instead of shaming and blaming me, they embraced me and went to war in prayer for our family. For three years, we met weekly as they prayed every verse of the book of Ephesians over our family and mentored me in re-building our marriage. Once we began implementing the simple truths of God's Word in our marriage and later in our parenting, transformation took place. We're still the same strong-willed people, but for four decades we've experienced victory after victory in the battle for our home. Today, we minister to families around the world and share the life-giving truths from God's Word that set us free. Our problem became our platform. Our fight led to our freedom.

I love this fight story. It's one that declares trust in God and His provision after the honeymoon fades and the messy middle shows up. As we fight for our marriages, what we believe about marriage and how we live out the marriage covenant are vital to the threats that come against our marriages. We must fight against these forces and against ourselves (at times), while we fight for our marriages. We fight for faithfulness. We fight for our children and their children. We fight for our homes to be a place of God's grace and peace. We also fight for bliss!

"Do not be afraid of them. Remember the Lord, who is great and awesome, and fight for... your wives, and your homes."

MARITAL BLISS

Marital bliss – is it possible? I come from a strong heritage of marriage. My wife's parents have been married 56 years while my parents recently celebrated 61 years of marriage. Julee and I have recently celebrated 26 years. I am thankful that I have come to this fight with a great foundation established. This may be your back story, or it may not. Either way, I believe that marital bliss is available to you.

What do you believe about marriage?

Marital bliss is based on five core values that we must hold fast to. They are practical, doable, and possible for you to deploy today. They will help you prepare for marriage if you aren't yet married, and help you fight for your marriage if you are. Here are the five core values that I want to touch on.

B – Belief – What I believe about marriage matters.

L – Love – The true love that we learn from the Scripture says, "I will never leave you or forsake you." This is the model that God demonstrates for us and the standard that he sets for us to share with our spouse.

I – Intentionality – Intentionality is a mindset, seeing every single day as an opportunity to build your marriage.

S – Service – Service is the action arm of an intentional mind, as it demonstrates that our highest calling is to build up the home by serving my spouse.

S – Sex – Sex in the marriage bed is how we experience God's design of oneness and unity.

Let's spend a moment looking at each of these.

CORE VALUE #1 – BELIEF

What you believe about marriage matters. What are your beliefs about marriage?

First, marriage faces some significant opponents in our day and time. The first opponent is divorce on demand. This emerged from the family law act of 1969 which started in California and began to move across the country. Prior to this to get a divorce there had to be a fault – someone had to be at fault. Someone had messed up, had abandoned the covenant or had committed adultery. Divorce on demand proclaims, "It is nobody's fault. We are not compatible. We just don't want to be married anymore." There is no immorality, abandonment or abuse. They just don't want to be married any longer.

This mindset is a threat because there will be days or even seasons when all you can fathom is being out of your marriage. So, let me ask you what do you believe about no fault divorce?

Another opponent to marriage is the belief that marriage is a social institution, not a sacred one. When man gets to define and declare through legislation or the courts how to define marriage, we have lost our way. Before there was government and before there were laws, God had instituted the family through the covenant or marriage. God has established marriage.

A third opponent to marriage is co-habitation. Who needs marriage? For many, it is practical, as financially it just seems to make sense. But God gave us standards to protect us. God gave us the covenant of marriage for a reason. When we circumvent that and take matters into our own hands, we are telling God, "Your ways are just not that important to me." Cohabitation is an opponent to marriage, and it is prevalent everywhere you turn. Fewer people are entering a covenant of marriage than ever before.

Add to these three opponents the popular culture's view of sex and marriage as a whole. If you aren't careful you will simply see marriage as archaic and unnecessary. But I believe that marriage doesn't just have opponents. I also believe it was given to us by God for so much good.

You see, the God who created us, gave marriage to us as a gift. He defines marriage for us. Notice this in Genesis 2:18-25:

> Then the Lord God said, "It is not good that the man should be alone; I will make him a helper fit for him." Now out of the ground the Lord God had formed every beast of the field and every bird of the heavens and brought them to the man to see what he would call them. And whatever the man called every living creature, that was its name. The man gave names to all livestock and to the birds of the heavens and to every beast of the field. But for Adam there was not found a helper fit for him. So the Lord God caused a deep sleep to fall upon the man, and while he slept took one of his ribs and closed up its place with flesh. And the rib that the Lord God had taken from the man he made into a woman and brought her to the man. Then the man said,
>
> "This at last is bone of my bones
> and flesh of my flesh;
> she shall be called Woman,
> because she was taken out of Man."
>
> Therefore a man shall leave his father and his mother and hold fast to his wife, and they shall become one flesh. And the man and his wife were both naked and were not ashamed.

After man names all of the animals two by two, we see that the Lord declares, "It is not good for man to be alone." I love how God takes action. He makes the man fall into a deep sleep, takes a rib, and he forms the amazing gift of woman. God gives her to the man.

God's gift to you, husbands, is a wife – God's perfect partner to fan into flame your strengths and to shore up your inadequacies. God in his providence gave to man a woman, and he gave to the woman a man. That is God's definition of marriage.

Not only does God have a definition of marriage, God also has a design for marriage. We see this in Genesis 2:24 which says, "Therefore a man shall leave his father and his mother and hold fast to his wife, and they shall become one flesh."

Now if you are like me and like to underline or make notes, I would circle two terms here: hold fast and one flesh. God's design for marriage is Oneness! Unity! You will be united! You will be one. In God's math, one plus one equals one. God's design for your marriage is that you would be one; that you would be unified. That's Genesis chapter two. But then you turn the page to Genesis chapter three, and you see unity disrupted and the very reason we must fight for our marriages appears. As much as I believe that God wants unity and oneness for your marriage, I also believe Satan wants to disrupt God's desire for your marriage. Satan wants to disrupt your unity.

God gave Adam to Eve and Eve to Adam. They are living in unity, then along comes the snake. He slithers in and says, "You know God has created this whole deal for you but He is selling you short. He's got other things in mind." When Satan comes in, he brings lies into their relationship that caused separation. That is what the enemy did -- he brought a lie into the relationship to separate them and that's what he does to us today.

Satan does this through some of the opponents I've just laid out. That is not exhaustive – there are plenty. But he brings lies into our relationship to take that which is one, try to tear it apart, and create disunity. If you are married Satan hates you and hates your marriage covenant. He wants nothing more than for your marriage covenant to be destroyed. He can't wait to see you calling that divorce lawyer. He can't wait to see you in the courts. He can't wait to just sit there and laugh with all his minions, "Ha-ha - there is another one! Marital bliss – that is a lie!" He can't wait to disrupt the unity that God has for you. So how, knowing these things, do we walk in God's design for our marriage?

This is where the rest of the core values of marriage are lived out.

CORE VALUE #2 – LOVE

The true love that we learn from the Scripture says, "I will never leave you or forsake you." In 1 Corinthians 12:31b – 13:8a, we see this beautiful poetic declaration about the power of love in one's life. Look at what Paul writes to the church in Corinth.

And I will show you a still more excellent way.

If I speak in the tongues of men and of angels, but have not love, I am a noisy gong or a clanging cymbal. And if I have prophetic powers, and understand all mysteries and all knowledge, and if I have all faith, so as to remove mountains, but have not love, I am nothing. If I give away all I have, and if I deliver up my body to be burned, but have not love, I gain nothing.

Love is patient and kind; love does not envy or boast; it is not arrogant or rude. It does not insist on its own way; it is not irritable or resentful; it does not rejoice at wrongdoing, but rejoices with the truth. Love bears all things, believes all things, hopes all things, endures all things.

Love never ends.

The New International Version translation says of verse eight, "Love never fails." I love that bold promise. I love the length and breadth and depth of that declaration. So, what does this love look like? If you are reading the Greek, you would see the word agape. Agape never fails. The Greeks had three words for love. The first is eros – that is the pleasure-filled erotic experience. Then there is phileo, which is a brotherly fraternal type of love. Then there is agape. Agape is the expensive, sacrificial, demonstration of a desire to be in an intimate relationship regardless of one's response.

In the Old Testament Hebrew, it is the term "hesed" and it speaks of covenant-keeping faithfulness. So, this agape, this "hesed", is authored by and demonstrated by God.

How did God express agape to you and to me? The cross! It was extremely expensive, such that it cost Him His Son. It was sacrificial because He laid down His life. It was unconditional as the invitation is for any to come. It was a demonstration regardless of a response. The cross is God's proactive declaration of His love for us. This love is the love that never fails. In essence it sets its face and remains. It is proactive as it is a decision. It's set out there regardless of emotion or the roller coaster of life. It is consistent. It is constant. It is not based on someone's reaction to it. Agape never fails.

Gary Smalley tells a story about an old couple. This couple had been married 60 plus years. The husband still had his health in his mid 80's but his wife has declined tremendously and lived in an assisted living center. She had Alzheimer's disease. She didn't recognize him, know him, or know his name. Yet every single day, at the crack of dawn, he entered her room. He wanted to be there when she woke. Every single day he cared for her and nurtured her. He would comb her hair, bathe her, and feed her. But she was vicious to him. She had no idea who he was. Every single day, he waited until she was just about to fall asleep. He would give her a kiss on the cheek and say, "I will see you in the morning." Then he would walk out of the room and go home.

On this one evening, as he was walking by the nurses' station, the head nurse said to him, "Sir, we just want to affirm you and acknowledge how amazing your care is for your wife. But we also want to take a burden off you. You see your wife is in good care. She is in good hands. We want you to know that if you have some other things to do with your time, if you have some other situations that you need to look after, or some other errands you need to run, we have it covered."

This gracious man told them, "You are so kind. Thank you! But please understand that this is not about me and my time. This is about a vow I made. You see I made a promise to my wife well over 60 years ago, that for better or worse, in sickness and in health, till death do us part, that I would love her."

This is agape. This kind of love cannot be returned. It can't be reciprocated. God already knows this and yet He loves anyway. This is how God first loved us, and it is how we are to love. This covenant love will guarantee your marital success. This love never fails!

If you want that to be the testimony of your covenant relationship, how do you do it? How do you walk in it?

I've got one word for you. This one word deployed by both husband and wife into their marriage daily, through intentionality, service, and sex, will transform your marriage. This one word, lived out, has the power to resurrect your dead marriage.

Are you ready? Do I have your attention? It is the word, honor. Honor! Gary Smalley teaches that honor is the foundation of every healthy relationship. To honor is to esteem, to give weight to, and to prioritize. To honor is to highly value. You see when we worship God, we are esteeming Him. We are giving him priority. We are giving him value. We are placing Him in his rightful place. To honor anyone else, God must be at the focal point of honor in our lives. He must be the first that we honor.

Then, we are to honor our spouse. We are to communicate over and over, "I honor you." It is easy to honor when you are in sync, isn't it? You are both marching to the same beat, you are doing the same thing, you're going in the same direction and it is easy to honor then. When you really get tested is when the response isn't what you want. But we must remember that agape is love and honor declared, regardless of response.

Before we unpack this further, let me give you a formula for failing at every single relationship. I can guarantee you failure in every relationship as well. Do you want to know how? Do you want to fail in your relationships? You dishonor the person in that relationship repeatedly and you will fail. It is not that hard. If you honor you are going to be fine. If you dishonor you will fail.

CORE VALUE #3 – INTENTIONALITY

Intentionality is a mindset that views every single day as an opportunity to build your marriage. Intentionality is the climate that allows honor to be expressed. What are some intentional things that you pursue in your marriage?

We try to get away at least once a year— just the two of us. We plan a four or five-night trip somewhere. We have no other agenda but to be together and enjoy one another's company. We do this just to continue to stoke the fire and flames of our marriage. We love the beach. Julee is a planner, so she gets online and hunts out something that will resonate with both of our hearts and then we book it, because once we have put the money down, we are invested.

Another intentional practice is that we have regular date nights. Some people are rigid about that – once a week. I think that is great. But for us, it is probably every three or four weeks where we get to go out to a nice dinner. Sometimes we may go shopping or to the movies. It is a great opportunity for us to stay connected. These are opportunities for connections. But intentionality declares that every single day is an opportunity for us to build our marriage. We do this through honor, by giving weight and worth to one another, and through a climate of blessing.

In 1 Peter 3, the Apostle Peter addresses relationships. He begins with wives and husbands and then takes it another step. He includes everyone in the congregation whether married or not. What follows is not just a lesson for your marriage. It is for relationships and how to do them well. 1 Peter 3:8-12 says:

> Finally, all of you, have unity of mind, sympathy, brotherly love, a tender heart, and a humble mind. Do not repay evil for evil or reviling for reviling, but on the contrary, bless, for to this you were called, that you may obtain a blessing. For

"Whoever desires to love life
and see good days,
let him keep his tongue from evil
and his lips from speaking deceit;
let him turn away from evil and do good;
let him seek peace and pursue it.
For the eyes of the Lord are on the righteous,
and his ears are open to their prayer.
But the face of the Lord is against those who do evil."

Choose Your Climate

A lot of people who are approaching retirement age begin to think and dream about where they will retire. In doing so, they are choosing the climate in which they want to live. Some people who have means are called snowbirds. They move from the north down to the south because they want to be in a warmer climate. They get to choose their climate.

Did you know that intentionality teaches us that we can choose the climate in which we live? Verses nine and ten shows us how. "Do not repay evil for evil or reviling for reviling, but on the contrary, bless, for to this you were called, that you may obtain a blessing. Whoever desires to love life and see good days, let him keep his tongue from evil and his lips from speaking deceit…"

The Apostle Peter is challenging followers of Jesus Christ to create a climate of blessing with our words. For you and me to create a climate of blessing, we must speak words of approval. We must speak words of affirmation. We must speak words of encouragement. We must speak well of others. That is what this idea of choosing your climate really is. It's to honor others with your words.

Three Levels of Living

There are three levels of living. Let's start at the bottom level. The bottom level is the satanic level of living. When good happens to you, you repay it with evil because your heart is nothing but evil. I don't think that is you, but that is the bottom level of living. When someone blesses you and you repay them with evil, it is because your heart is hard and darkened.

The next level of living is the human level of living. When good is done to us, we need to do good back. When evil is done to us, we go back to the Old Testament, "an eye for an eye, a tooth for a tooth. Here it comes!" We clench the fist, and we repay evil with evil, insult with insult.

In marriage, how do you communicate with one another? When it is good, I hope you communicate good. But what about when it is tense, difficult, stressful, or bad? What is your climate? Is it blessing? Are you returning curse for curse, insult for insult, and evil for evil?

What climate are you creating in your home? See you can internationally choose blessing every single time. That takes you to this third level of living: godly living. 1 Peter 3 says this is what you were called to do. Even though we may be insulted and we may be hurt, we are to choose godly living which means to bless even when we are cursed.

Are there times in your relationship when you are speaking words of forgiveness? Are you speaking words of grace daily? Are you speaking words of encouragement? Are you speaking words of affirmation? Are you speaking words of kindness? The tongue is powerful. It contains the words of life and death. What is the climate of your speech? Intentionality says today is an opportunity to create a climate of blessing. I want to challenge you to intentionally choose a climate of honor with your words.

CORE VALUE #4 – SERVICE

Service is the action arm of an intentional mind. It demonstrates that our highest calling is to build up the home by serving our spouse. If we intentionally establish a climate of honor with our words, service is the means by which we create intentional actions that honor our spouse. How do we grab hold of service?

One saying that helps me serve my wife and kids well is: The way up is down! If you want to build intentionally toward bliss, you must lower yourself. Jesus demonstrates this for us as well as teaching this to us. In Matthew 20 James and John's mom comes out of nowhere to ask Jesus a question. She says, "Jesus, when you enter into your kingdom, grant it that my boys can sit on your right and on your left."

In other words, she is asking him for a great position, and for great authority. Jesus' response is like, "Ma'am, do you even know what you are asking?" Then he turns to them and says, "Guys, do you even know what she is saying? Can you handle this place?" When you keep reading the story, you see this request really frustrates the other disciples. It says in Matthew 20:24-28.

> And when the ten heard it, they were indignant at the two brothers. But Jesus called them to him and said, "You know that the rulers of the Gentiles lord it over them, and their great ones exercise authority over them. It shall not be so among you. But whoever would be great among you must be your servant, and whoever would be first among you must be your slave, even as the Son of Man came not to be served but to serve, and to give his life as a ransom for many."

Why did the other 10 disciples get upset with James and John? The simple answer is that they didn't want to be lorded over. They wanted a shot at those positions themselves. They didn't want James and John to have authority over them. They wanted authority.

That's the model of leadership that they saw with Rome – with the Gentiles. That's the model of leadership that they all knew. It's that old saying about the golden rule, "That he who has the gold makes the rules."

Yet, what does Jesus say to this? Verses 26 and 27 state:

> It shall not be so among you. But whoever would be great among you must be your servant, and whoever would be first among you must be your slave…

Jesus has just redefined leadership and greatness all at the same time.

- Do you want to be a great husband? Great! Don't look at the way of the world or even the way your dad was a husband to get your playbook. Instead, lay your life down for your wife. That's what greatness looks like in the kingdom of God.

- Do you want to be a great wife? Great! Honor your husband through your speech, your humility and your respect, because the way up is down! Greatness in God's sight is found and established through serving.

So, what are practical ways you serve? How are you found serving your spouse every single day? I do something simple that I love to do for my wife each day. It's just my little hack to declare to her that I am there to serve her every day. My hack to remind me to serve is to make her coffee for her, whether that's on the weekday, as she heads out the door to be at work by 7:30 a.m., or on Saturday when I am up before her, and I hear her stirring. It is my joy and honor to make her coffee. It's my declaration to her that I am here to serve you today.

Now, the important thing that ensures that this is authentic is I strive to continue my service throughout the day, as the way up is…DOWN!

You are getting a hold of it now. You can begin to do this today and every single day moving forward. The more we honor and serve our husband or wife, the more intimacy we are guaranteed.

CORE VALUE #5 – SEX

Sex in the marriage bed is how we experience God's design of oneness and unity. Now some reading this may say, "Why are you talking about sex?" Well, first and foremost, because everyone else is. You cannot check out of the grocery store without running into a magazine like Allure, with headlines on the cover that read, "Get the sexiest eyes ever." Then there is Glamour, whose cover reads,

"Everything you wanted to know about sex, guilt free shopping, easy beauty and lots of guys, plus, hot insider gossip."

In our culture, people hold up sex as a God. It saturates the airways whether it is music, television, movies, or social media advertising. It is easily accessible, as false sex with a two-dimensional image is rampant. As a matter of fact, the pornography industry brings in $60 billion a year with $12 billion right here in North American. We have made sex our idol.

Why is sex our idol? Because that is where we spend our money as a nation, and Jesus said, "...where your treasure is, your heart will be also." [10] It is what is in the locker room. It is the coarse joke that we talk about. It is what comedians make their living talking about. That is why we are talking about sex. Not only is it a core value that leads to marital bliss if we properly understand it, but we must understand that in our culture, it has been made a diety.

Our God has said very plainly, "You shall have no other gods before me," and if sex is your idol, I want to invite you to come to the cross for forgiveness. Because that pathway only leads to brokenness, it leads to hurt, it leads to shame, and it leads to loss. Jesus came to set us free.

Others reading this may see sex as icky and something we shouldn't be talking about. Whether from your upbringing or your experience, when sex is brought up it brings up all kinds of thoughts. Some of those thoughts are negative. Maybe something happened to you, so this brings up pain. Somewhere along the way, sex gained a negative connotation that created a barrier from ever enjoying real intimacy in the marriage bed. Your upbringing, your experience, or something maybe that you did willfully, brought shame into your life, and you've never broken through and had your hurts healed. If that is you, I am so sorry about your experience. I also want to encourage you to come to the cross of the Lord Jesus Christ, because He is the one who sets us free. Hand him that pain, brokenness or shame and ask Him to renew your mind in this area.

The word of God teaches us that sex is a gift for oneness and intimacy. When believers have the proper understanding and walk in that, they resemble the picture of Jesus Christ and His Church. It is a very fulfilling gift.

Tim Keller in his book, The Meaning of Marriage, says that:

> "Sex is for whole-life, self-giving and perhaps the most powerful God-created way, to help you give your entire self to another human being. Sex is God's pointed way for two people to reciprocally say to one another, I belong completely, permanently, exclusively to you." [11]

Sex in the marriage covenant is intended to be a gift. The writer of Proverbs warns his son against adultery, then instructs him to be satisfied in his wife, all the days of his life. More than satisfaction, he challenges his son to be intoxicated with her love. Notice these words as we seek to be stewards of the gift of sex in marriage. Proverbs 5:15-19 says:

> Drink water from your own cistern,
>   flowing water from your own well.
> Should your springs be scattered abroad,
>   streams of water in the streets?
> Let them be for yourself alone,
>   and not for strangers with you.
> Let your fountain be blessed,
>   and rejoice in the wife of your youth,
>   a lovely deer, a graceful doe.
> Let her breasts fill you at all times with delight;
>   be intoxicated always in her love.

You see we are stewards of the gifts that God has given us. So how are we to steward this wonderful gift? This is where we look to Paul's instruction in 1 Corinthians six and seven.

Sex as an Idol

Now let me give you some context. The city of Corinth was a major, amazing city. It was a place we would want to visit. At its zenith, when Paul wrote this letter to the church of Corinth, it was the political center of the region. Corinth was the trade center and the center of Greek philosophy. There were all kinds of amazing things going on in Corinth. This was the place to be.

Corinth was also known for its worship. There were 12 temples in which one could go and engage in pagan worship. There was a synagogue there established by the Jews of the community as well. But the most renowned place of worship was the temple of Aphrodite. This temple employed 1,000 priests and priestesses, male and female, where people could come and freely engage in pagan worship with sexual idolatry.

The Spiritual Should Govern the Physical

In this context, Paul gives us some significant teaching. He acknowledges sex can become an idol, sex can be seen as awful, or it can be seen as a gift. Now, the over-arching principle is that our relationship with Jesus Christ must govern our physical experience.

Corinth was a place of great sexual immorality. In fact, to "Corinthianize" was to commit sexually immorality. Paul said to the church in Corinth:

> "All things are lawful for me," but not all things are helpful. "All things are lawful for me," but I will not be dominated by anything. "Food is meant for the stomach and the stomach for food"—and God will destroy both one and the other. The body is not meant for sexual immorality, but for the Lord, and the Lord for the body. And God raised the Lord and will also raise us up by his power. Do you not know that your bodies are members of Christ? Shall I then take the members of Christ and make them members of a prostitute? Never! Or do you not

know that he who is joined to a prostitute becomes one body with her? For, as it is written, "The two will become one flesh." But he who is joined to the Lord becomes one spirit with him. Flee from sexual immorality. Every other sin a person commits is outside the body, but the sexually immoral person sins against his own body. 1 Corinthians 6:8-12

There are a couple of big ideas here: Number one, since you are in Jesus Christ, that relationship must govern what you do physically. Number two is the call to honor God with our bodies. Verse 13b says:

> The body is not meant for sexual immorality, but for the Lord, and the Lord for the body.

This includes adultery, fornication, pornography, multiple sex partners, and sex outside the covenant of marriage. Your body was not made for that. This is not the master's design. Sex has been perverted and then exalted as a god. As members of Christ, our bodies are members of Christ's body. It says in verse 15:

> Do you not know that your bodies are members of Christ?

Verse 17 echoes that, stating:

> But he who is joined to the Lord becomes one spirit with him.

Verses 19 and 20 then say:

> Or do you not know that your body is a temple of the Holy Spirit within you, whom you have from God? You are not your own, for you were bought with a price. So glorify God in your body.

In other words, the Apostle instructs them to quit going down to those temples because your body is the temple, the temple of the Lord.

Sin Against Ourselves

Another thing we see here is that sexual sin is a sin against our own self. I can lie, cheat, and steal. I can say words against you. Those types of sin are against another. But when we sin sexually, we sin against our own body. There are consequences that go along with that. You see the sin against the body damages my outlook on life. It hurts my conscience. It damages my sense of self-worth.

What Paul is saying is: "Why would you want to do that? Let your relationship with Jesus Christ govern what you do physically. Instead, honor God with your body. Quit seeing sex as God. Yes, you live in an idolatrous land, but you are to have no gods before him. Stop walking in those ways. Repent and return to the Lord."

Sex as Disgusting, Evil, or Not to Be Enjoyed

Paul also deals with idea that sex isn't enjoyable. Did you know the idea that sex is disgusting, has been in the church, since its foundation? As a matter of fact, many of the church fathers, like Tertullian and Ambrose were said to prefer the extinction of the human race rather than the continued sexual intercourse of a couple – those in a covenant marriage. Origen, a church father, was so convinced of the evils of sexual pleasure that he not only allegorized the Song of Songs to make it say something it didn't say, but he also took a knife and castrated himself.

Gregory Anissi taught that Adam and Eve were created without sexual desire. You can continue to trace this disdain for sex in the church through the 1200, 1300, and 1400's. Greek philosophy had entered into the equation and had informed the believers in Corinth as to what their body was and wasn't. To some the body was just evil matter, and if it is evil, some said, "Well let's just go live it up. All that I am really to worry about is my soul and my spirit since my body is evil. I may as well just go and gratify my body's pleasures." Others may have said, "If my body is evil and the urges of my body are evil, then I must punish my body." So, one of the questions the church at Corinth wrote to Paul about was celibacy. Now, Paul, himself was celibate – a single man who does not engage in any sex acts. He affirms this celibate, single life in verse seven and following, when he says:

> Now concerning the matters about which you wrote: "It is good for a man not to have sexual relations with a woman." 1 Corinthians 7:1

So, if you have the gift of singleness, you will see this in verse seven and following, as there is a call to stay celibate. God can really use that and use your time to do amazing things through you. But understand he doesn't prefer celibacy within the context of marriage. This is what Paul is bringing forth in chapter seven, verses two and following:

> But because of the temptation to sexual immorality, each man should have his own wife and each woman her own husband. The husband should give to his wife her conjugal rights, and likewise the wife to her husband. For the wife does not have authority over her own body, but the husband does. Likewise the husband does not have authority over his own body, but the wife does. Do not deprive one another, except perhaps by agreement for a limited time, that you may devote yourselves to prayer; but then come together again, so that Satan may not tempt you because of your lack of self-control.

Here are some things that I have heard around the table in my office talking to a husband or wife about their struggles in marriage. I've heard things like:

- "She only allows me to be intimate with her about twice a year."
- "We have not had sex – he withholds it… We haven't had sex in at least 18 months."

A friend of mine said, "Yeah, I have friends going through a divorce. They haven't had sex in six years."

This is a very real issue – sex as icky; sex as evil; sex as not to be enjoyed; sex as that which brings up all kinds of hurt and pain.

God did not design you to be in a marriage covenant and be celibate! But in talking about this with my wife, I asked her about sermons on marriage and sex in the church. She said, "Sermons on this topic are all from the perspective of the man."

Yet here Paul comes alongside the wife and says, "Guys, lend me your attention! You are to serve her sexually!" The word here in the Greek New Testament is "ofelia," and many translations render it the word, "duty." When we talk about duty, we give sex a negative connotation.

Linda Dillo and Lorraine Pendas, in their book, Intimate Issues: Conversations Woman to Woman, unpack this word for us. They say that the word duty in English carries with it the idea of an unpleasant task. But it is not the conferring of a favor with the idea that says, "Oh, I will accommodate you when or if I feel like it." The actual message conveyed by the Greek word is that of a debt. It is the payment of a debt that is owed. That is what this scripture is teaching. Notice this in verse three.

> The husband should give to his wife her conjugal rights, and likewise the wife to her husband.

A prominent idea in Corinth at that time was that sex between the husband and wife was just for procreation. Christians even practiced this. Therefore, the wife had no rights. She couldn't find pleasure in the marriage bed.

Yet the husband had all kinds of rights, especially sexually. In that culture and in that city, the husband would say, "See ya' hon," and he would go right on down to one of those temples and engage in sexual prostitution for his pleasure.

Yet, the wife was longing to be with her husband to experience this oneness. He wasn't open to meeting her needs or considering that she has any rights whatsoever. That's messed up!

In first-century Christianity, Paul is saying: "Guys, quit seeing sex as god. Quit going down and engaging in temple worship because your body is the temple. Further, within the context of marriage, God has given you a perfect complement and she too has rights and needs and it is your duty and obligation to meet her needs."

Now, stick with me for just another minute. Husbands, your wife's needs are very different than your needs. You have heard the saying, "Sex begins in the kitchen." That's true. It begins in the kitchen. It doesn't begin in just a few minutes, but it is something that develops all day long.

You see, when you (B) believe properly, and you (L) love correctly, and you are (I) intentional, and you begin to (S) serve over and over and over again…guess what? There is going to be more (S) sex. There is going to be better sex, there is going to be good sex. There is going to be oneness. When honor is present in word and deed, and this is the climate you both set, one to another, bliss is the result. But the key to this level of living is recognizing that your biggest challenge to overcome is yourself.

TOO MUCH OF ME IN ME

I say this all the time and unfortunately, all too often it rings true. The reality of why Julee and I don't live at this level always is that I have a problem. I have too much of me in me. I would suspect that may be your problem too. We have too much selfishness, unresolved conflict, lessons of what not to do that we learned from our parents, and the ultimate destroyer of relationships: pride. I am the problem in my marriage. I get in my own way. I trip up my own desires for my home and marriage and must go back and repair what I have been trying to build. That's why we must fight for ourselves to cultivate our character and continually surrender our hearts to Jesus Christ so we can fight for our marriage.

As we close out this chapter, check out Allison's fight story as she reflects on a 20 year journey of fighting for her marriage.

My fight story is about marriage. I went out on my first date with my (now) husband the night before college started my freshman year at Texas A&M. We were married three weeks after we graduated. We had our first child four years later, a daughter. Our second child came 19 months later, and our third child two years after that. By the time I had three children three and a half years and under, I was drowning.

I was all in on parenting and holding on to marriage by a thin thread. We loved each other, but it was so hard to connect when we were both working hard at two different things. But we fought for our marriage.

Every time I would bring up working on our marriage, Robert was all in. Every single time the enemy was right there crouching at our door, waiting to pounce. We never got into any serious marital trouble, but it was always a fight. We always knew there was something more that God had for marriage than just surviving.

Through the years, we have chosen to go to marital counseling several different times. The real change came when we went to counseling, not as a couple, but individually. We showed up with our problems and said, "Help me change. Help me see where my blind spots are. Show me the human ways I think about an enormous God." God showed up. It's still messy, but it's SO much better. 20 years in, it's SO much better. The relationship, the intimacy, the friendship, and the partnership – God is SO good. He took all those years of prayers and tears, and He's turning them in to something beautiful.

Sometimes I wallow in "20 wasted years," but then I'm reminded of Psalm 18:30 that says, "As for God, His way is perfect; the word of the Lord is flawless, He is a shield for all who take refuge in Him." He holds our whole life in His hands and not a moment is ever a mistake.

REFLECTION QUESTIONS:

If you are married, take a few minutes to discuss with your spouse the meaning of each letter of BLISS.

1. What did you discover in B?

2. How is God's love (L) mirrored in your marriage?

3. How does the culture's idea of love creep into your marriage?

4. Which of the letters I, S, and S do you do well in your marriage? Which letter needs work?

5. What can you do intentionally every day to serve your spouse?

CHAPTER 5

Fighting for Change: Go to the Broken Places

David Glenn's fight story involves going to the broken places of his heart, and coming to the place of complete surrender. David says:

My fight story began when God answered my prayer to heal me from areas of my flesh that I could see in my life. On January 1, 1993, I asked the Lord to purge me from fear and insecurity, the love of money, and a critical tongue. I asked to "bear more fruit" for Him. Within six weeks of that prayer, the Heavenly Vine-Dresser took His pruning shears and cut away my job as a petroleum geophysicist. I got laid off! For a guy who is fearful and insecure, this was like cutting my arm off! Denise had just quit her job as a teacher at our church school, where we had our three girls enrolled in a very expensive private school education!

This was a major financial, emotional, and spiritual blow for us. We went away on a weekend getaway to cry and hear from God.

Barry Landrum suggested I attend a seminar he had just attended called, "The Exchange Life Seminar." My "spiritual antenna" was up and ready to hear from God, and He spoke! As I studied and read, the reality of my need to "go to the cross" sank in. God was saying something powerful. I grew uncomfortable as I realized going to the cross "means surrender with no reservations- not friends, family, profession, future, or possessions." If we are dead serious, we are going to be seriously dead! It was a surrender giving permission to the Father to take me to the cross. Galatians 2:20 spoke the most to me: "I have been crucified with Christ and I no longer live, but Christ lives in me. The life I live in the body, I live by faith in the Son of God, who loved me and gave himself for me."

I had to die to my self-nature. On March 11, 1993, I got on my knees and prayed the Selfer's Prayer, giving up trying to live my life in my own strength, and receiving the full resurrection power of Christ. It was a major spiritual breakthrough for me. I made Jesus my Savior at 11, my Lord at 29 (after my near marriage disaster) but made Him my LIFE on this day!

What does victory look like? It looks like this, "I want to know Christ and the power of his resurrection..." (Philippians 3:10). Victory, the abundant life that Jesus talks about in John chapter 10 and the resurrection power, begins AFTER we go to the cross. My spiritual life and the life of our ministry took off like a rocket, after this transformation. The "Freedom for Fathers Bible Study" was written based on this transforming experience. This fight was the worst and best experience in my whole life! Christ's grace IS sufficient!

What broken places are you being called to? Whether it's in your heart, your family of origin story, or a burden to do ministry where few others have gone, we cannot take this journey alone.

BROKEN HOMES LEAD TO BROKEN NEIGHBORHOODS AND BROKEN CITIES

"What if Houston had no bad neighborhoods?" Those were the words of Kirk Craig, CEO of Agape Development Ministries in Houston, Texas. As we shared a meal at Grace's Table on Kirby, Kirk's eyes were full of passion. I could tell that his heart still raced for the peace of God over every part of our city.

What if Houston had no bad neighborhoods? That question stuck with me that day. I'm still carrying it around. When you fight for the city, you fight for neighborhoods. When you fight for neighborhoods, you fight for churches. When you fight for churches, you fight for the home. That's why we must fight for the church. The church is to lead the way in fighting for our communities and homes. At least, that's what I have observed from Kirk and Amanda Craig and David and Melissa Hill. Take a few minutes to grasp the story of Agape Development Ministries.

Houston's Greater Third Ward has a rich spiritual history. For many decades there have been faithful saints ministering the grace of the Gospel of Jesus. In the summer of 1998, a young woman came to serve in Houston's Greater Third Ward between semesters of college. Though not unfamiliar with poverty and missions, she was captivated by the ministry of God's people who lived as neighbors in the community, not just 9-to-5 employees. For a summer, her life became intertwined with the life of the inner city- its children, its youth, its single mothers, and its faithful grandmothers. She met pastors and elders in a local church who modeled the Gospel in a way that touched her heart.

That summer of walking through the joys and pains with her neighbors would forever change the lives of Amanda Van Zandt Craig, her future husband Kirk Craig, and their four children. With the capable guidance of a local board of directors and the loving partnership of these families, God began to grow the Agape Community in the OST/South Union neighborhood and

in 2005 Agape Development was founded. God graciously provided the partnership with David and Melissa Hill who had been
faithfully serving as urban missionaries long before the Craig's
arrived. David and Melissa, along with their children, lived in the
community and modeled the type of ministry Amanda had seen
that first summer.

Though the ministry's first programs served only young adults,
God opened the way for other programs to reach our neighbors.
The original staff and neighbors of Sean, Emily, Jenny, Anne,
Jessie, Derrick, Nikki, Renae, Ava, Terry, and David have been
followed by so many others who have joined in the gospel work
together. Starting with children's ministry, Agape Development
began adding program offerings to encompass teens, young adult
transitional housing, community gardens, adult employment and
discipleship, community celebrations and clean-ups as well.

In the most recent years, Agape Development added Social
Enterprise and Housing offerings to community transformation
efforts. The businesses provide meaningful employment and
discipleship to residents of the 77021 zip code, while sustaining
their operations through earned income. Lawn care, fence building, siding, roofing, and remodeling services have been among
the skills that residents learn along with family leadership and
financial management. In an effort to retain leadership, Agape
Homes has designed and will build single family houses for sale at
an affordable price for neighbors. This represents lasting leadership pipelines in our community. Agape Development is grate-
ful for the church's historic foundations in the community and
proud of our own history. However, we are even more excited
about the future in this neighborhood. [12]

VISION LEADS TO TRANSFORMATION

Burdens lead to vision. Vision leads to transformation when leaders
are willing to act. That's the Agape Development story. In the story of
Ezra and Nehemiah, you see this as well – God is raising up leaders to

go to the broken and desolate places. In so many ways, these are some of the best kingdom stories we tell throughout history. These are stories of people who went where no one else was willing to go. They are the stories of Mark and Susie who planted the first church by the International Mission Board behind the iron curtain. They are the stories of Chad and Ashlie who felt compelled to leave Houston and move to Morocco, then on to Amsterdam, because of the call of the gospel, to share the good news with North Africans. It's Keith and Tricia whom God has called to reach the Sudanese people, or DJ and Kelly who moved into a war-torn country half-way around the world to share the love of Jesus with these who have never heard.

People with pioneering spirits go to broken places to pick up the pieces. Dorretta and Zeral Brown began their gospel work in the Dominican Republic in 1947. As Zeral started to preach the gospel, he also discipled and trained new converts to preach the Gospel in their own villages. A few years later, an eight-year-old boy named Rudy was captured by the gospel shared by one of these original converts and was called to preach. Meanwhile, the Browns were called to ministry in Cuba for a few years, but after Castro's regime took hold, they returned to the Dominican Republic with TIME Ministries. Zeral and Dorretta re-connected with Pastor Rudy. They designed and built a wooden portable chapel. With the help of short-term mission groups, they have constructed over 400 buildings to date, which enabled new church plants all over the island nation.

At the same time, Zeral and Dorretta worked with Pastor Rudy to plant the Iglesia Bautista Quiqueyana (IBQ) in northern Santo Domingo. As his congregation grew, Rudy saw the need to continue to reach out into the greater city by discipling converts and training more leaders to teach and preach. As a result, many more churches were planted in the Santo Domingo area, and beyond.

Dorretta and Zeral's daughter, Joanna Berry, was living in Texas and working with STCH Ministries as a counselor when she began to wrestle with how STCH Ministries might get involved in international mission work in the Dominican Republic alongside Pastor Rudy. She saw great needs with the education system, orphans and other systemic issues that plague the poor. In 2006 STCH Ministries began to invest heavily into this partnership while working out of the Quisqueyana Baptist Church to lift an entire city. Activating Texas churches to get involved became Joanna's passion. In time, STCH Ministries began to offer family mission trips to these church partners, using their passion to build schools and churches, desks, beds, conduct Vacation Bible Schools and operate medical clinics. To date, STCH Ministries, the Iglesia Bautista Quisqueyana, and US mission teams have helped to plant more than ten churches, constructed or expanded eight Christian schools, and built four orphanages. Through their sponsorship programs they have also sponsored over 400 children for elementary and high school, and 48 students for their university studies. STCH Ministries is now expanding its work into other countries in Latin America, believing God for more restoration and gospel impact.

EARLY FAITH-FILLED ADOPTERS

The great rebuilding story of the temple as found in Ezra involves two waves of people who took the four-month journey to return to Jerusalem. Both groups went to broken places. I believe we can learn a lot from their journey. They had a pioneering spirit and a willingness to put themselves on the line because they believed that what was lying in ruin was worth rebuilding.

What broken places are you being called to return to? These may be broken places in your heart from past relationships. Your broken place may be generational sin that is rearing its head in your home just as it did in the home of your upbringing. These broken places may be insecurities, wounds from your parents, or unresolved conflict in your marriage. It may be a call to work with the homeless and the poor, to teach in a low-performing school, or a move to another continent. How is God showing you your gifts and calling to make a difference in that particular place in this particular time? As you fight for yourself, your home, your church, and your city, are you willing to go where the foundations need to be repaired and where the walls are torn down? Ezra 2:1-9 sets the table for the rest of the chapter. In Ezra 2, 49,897 people are accounted for through their head of household. They will return to Judah, the southern kingdom of Israel. Each will live in his own town. Some are priests and Levites. Others are gatekeepers and temple servants. Some are simply sons and daughters who have dreamed about returning to their inheritance and rebuilding their lives. Notice how these early adopters are introduced to us.

> Now these were the people of the province who came up out of the captivity of those exiles whom Nebuchadnezzar the king of Babylon had carried captive to Babylonia. They returned to Jerusalem and Judah, each to his own town. They came with Zerubbabel, Jeshua, Nehemiah, Seraiah, Reelaiah, Mordecai, Bilshan, Mispar, Bigvai, Rehum, and Baanah.

> The number of the men of the people of Israel: the sons of Parosh, 2,172. The sons of Shephatiah, 372. The sons of Arah, 775. The sons of Pahath-moab, namely the sons of Jeshua and Joab, 2,812. The sons of Elam, 1,254. The sons of Zattu, 945.

You get the picture here. This list goes on for almost 70 verses detailing those who returned. What we don't see here, but that we need to see, is that these were faith-filled people. Psalm 126 details for us the songs in their hearts as they returned to see Jerusalem restored.

> When the Lord restored the fortunes of Zion,
>   we were like those who dream.
> Then our mouth was filled with laughter,
>   and our tongue with shouts of joy;
> then they said among the nations,
>   "The Lord has done great things for them."
> The Lord has done great things for us;
>   we are glad.
> Restore our fortunes, O Lord,
>   like streams in the Negeb!
> Those who sow in tears
>   shall reap with shouts of joy!
> He who goes out weeping,
>   bearing the seed for sowing,

shall come home with shouts of joy,
bringing his sheaves with him.

R. Jamieson says of the opening line of this Psalm, "The joy of those
returned from Babylon was ecstatic, and elicited the admiration even of
the heathen, as illustrating God's great power and goodness." [13] These
are a people who are being restored. They are laughing, shouting, and
declaring that the Lord has surely done great things for them. Their
prayers are for the Lord to restore them. They have sown with tears.
They shall reap with shouts of joy!

In this detailed account of those returning from exile to Jerusalem, the
writer of this book is going into great detail to make sure that all involved
understand that something greater than a caravan of 50,000 people is
headed south. This writer is taking attendance and noting very carefully
that each is going back to his own hometown. He is doing this so we can
connect the post-exilic Israel with pre-exilic Israel. M. Breneman states:

> Again, the author emphasized the continuity of God's covenant
> people. The material is presented to show God's providence in rees-
> tablishing the covenant community, in reordering its religious life
> (Neh. 8–10), and in revitalizing its cultural heritage (Neh. 11–13).
> Thus, the identification of the families and their place of origin was
> important for the self-identity of the people. They needed to recog-
> nize their roots in the preexilic Israelite community as reassurance
> that they were the continuation of God's redemptive plan, that
> God would not forsake them.

We can be glad that they did continue as God's covenant community and that they continued to be used in God's redemptive
plan. Through this community and their descendants, we have the
Scriptures, and through this community Jesus Christ came into
the world. Even though the community was practically unnoticed
in the world at that time, they constituted the center of God's
redemptive plan.

Sometimes Christians suffer from a "minority complex," thinking they are of little significance in present history. But the New Testament makes clear that the church, made up of true believers in Jesus Christ, is the center of God's attention and the chief means of fulfilling his mission in the world. We need to remember our heritage from generations of believers who have preceded us and understand the influence our decisions will have for the future. [14]

These in Ezra two had a pioneering spirit, probably similar to the spirit of Jim Elliott, who said, "He is no fool who gives up what he cannot keep to gain that which he cannot lose." Elliott was a martyr in the late 1950s trying to reach the Auca Indians of Ecuador. As the people of God, we must have a pioneering spirit to take the good news to broken places.

Wave #2

Ezra himself, isn't introduced to us until chapter seven, which is in 458 B.C. The temple rebuild was completed in 515 B.C. Ezra feels compelled to return to Jerusalem and shepherd the spiritual health of the people there. Warren Wiersbe says, "Ezra is presented to us as a godly and patriotic Jew who was a priest and a scribe (Ezra 7:1–6). He was a devoted student of the Scriptures and helped to restore the Law to the nation. He was also a man of prayer (8:21–23) and a man who was greatly burdened for the spiritual welfare of his people (9:3–4). His name means 'help.'" [15]

…this Ezra went up from Babylonia. He was a scribe skilled in the Law of Moses that the Lord, the God of Israel, had given, and the king granted him all that he asked, for the hand of the Lord his God was on him. Ezra 7:6

Now, look at verse 10.

For Ezra had set his heart to study the Law of the Lord, and to do it and to teach his statutes and rules in Israel.

From these two verses, we are introduced to a peak-performer. He's a leader. He is skilled. He boldly asked the king for assistance. He had set his heart to know the law of God, to live it out, and then to teach this to those who would listen.

Now, as I describe Ezra to you, I don't want you to think I am casting him in a negative light. That is not the case at all. I'm trying to highlight a man who was full of the Spirit of God and was zealous for the ways of the Lord. Informing people how they should live their lives takes a certain confidence and competence. It's not an easy task. But those who lead others to the things of God do it because they have tasted of the goodness of God over and against everything else and they want that for others. Those who lead others to the Lord, do so because they have been tasked, called, and empowered by God Himself to both walk by faith and lead others to do the same. Apparently, Ezra did this with all diligence, as the king granted him all that he asked for as he took this journey. He loaded him up and essentially gave him a blank check (see Ezra 7:11-26) to get what he needed and spend what was necessary to fulfill what was in his heart to do.

We need spiritual leaders today who are full of zeal for God. We need leaders today who are full of the Spirit of God,. We need leaders who are diligent with the resources entrusted to them. Ezra was using his gifts, training, experience, and God's favor upon him to lead people back to the house of the Lord.

Pastor Petr Samoylich is pastor of Riga Mission Baptist Church in Riga, Latvia. Petr has been described as the Billy Graham of Latvia. He hosts a teacher's conference every year, instructing public school teachers how to teach the Bible. After the fall of the Soviet Union, the Latvian government determined there was a need to teach children moral values. They decided to use the Holy Bible to do this even though there was zero spiritual intent. Petr has taken advantage of this opportunity to train public school teachers, because if they will get this training and teach these children, they will get extra compensation. Many teachers have professed Christ because of coming to the teachers training conference and because of teaching the Bible.

Petr also has a summer camp for kids. He loves to take kids to camp and show them the love of Jesus and the joy of the Lord. Pastor Petr always ensures that thirty percent of the children will come from orphanages. He has reached many children in this way through the years. Our church has had the privilege of partnering with him in Vacation Bible School for several years. He seeks to reach the children because he knows that they can impact their parents. Additionally, atheism is still steeped into the minds of many of the adults and so there is very little belief in God in Eastern European countries like Latvia.

Reaching out to children led Petr to Vecmilgravis, a blue-collar ship building town just on the outskirts of Riga. Petr discovered that the only church in this town was for Latvian speaking citizens, while over 90% of the residents of Vecmilgravis spoke Russian. He knew that he had to establish an evangelical church in this city. In 2011 Petr felt compelled to start a church on Sunday afternoons in Vecmilgravis meeting at the Latvian speaking Lutheran Church. This was the birth of the Riga New Evangelical Baptist Church. It is the first Russian speaking evangelical church in this community since before World War I. Petr began showing up and reaching out. He mobilized some of his youth to get involved. They hosted camps and Vacation Bible Schools. Petr found a facility and began to raise money. In 2014 he bought this location and began the remodeling, doing much of the construction with his own hands. Riga New Evangelical Baptist Church of Vecmilgravis continues to grow and thrive. Pastor Petr has faithfully been preaching each Sunday in two locations for the last 10 years.

Petr is building an evangelical witness to this community of some 85,000 Russian speaking Latvians so that they might know the hope of Jesus Christ. He believes this will be his greatest task and prays it outlives him, as he is fighting for an entire generation of Latvians to come to Jesus Christ. I have known Pastor Petr for many years. He is a man who is still full of zeal and the Holy Spirit and is very diligent with the resources entrusted to him.

AS YOU GO, DON'T GO ALONE

When you find yourself in the fight, you must fortify yourself with people of wisdom and strength. I have found that many people choose to keep quiet and not ask for help because they are afraid of what others will think of them when things come unraveled in their lives. In their efforts to manage the emerging challenge, they isolate and go it alone. But that's not what we see in the Scriptures. When Jesus went to the Garden of Gethsemane on the night He was betrayed, He took his disciples with Him and asked them to watch and pray with Him. We also see the Apostle Paul talking openly about his struggles and requesting prayer and support from the churches. Ezra does not want to wage this war alone. The last verse of Ezra 7 states:

> I took courage, for the hand of the Lord my God was on me, and I gathered leading men from Israel to go up with me

Unfortunately, as we set out to proactively make a difference or as we find ourselves on the defensive because a fight has been brought to us, we must recognize that not everyone will join us. Some will criticize us. Some will try to reprimand us. Some will simply not respond to the call to join the fight. Not everyone will go and not everyone will move.

Ezra encountered this as he began to recruit for the second wave of Jews who would return to Jerusalem. As you read Ezra chapter eight, you see that not enough Levites, the very people charged with tending to the temple and the word of God, were willing to go back to Jerusalem. Can you imagine this scenario? The very people who were to attend to the temple of God and His Word didn't seem willing to go? Notice what happens in Ezra 8.

> I gathered them to the river that runs to Ahava, and there we camped three days. As I reviewed the people and the priests, I found there none of the sons of Levi. Then I sent for Eliezer, Ariel, Shemaiah, Elnathan, Jarib, Elnathan, Nathan, Zechariah, and Meshullam, leading men, and for Joiarib and Elnathan,

who were men of insight, and sent them to Iddo, the leading man at the place Casiphia, telling them what to say to Iddo and his brothers and the temple servants at the place Casiphia, namely, to send us ministers for the house of our God. And by the good hand of our God on us, they brought us a man of discretion, of the sons of Mahli the son of Levi, son of Israel, namely Sherebiah with his sons and kinsmen, 18; also Hashabiah, and with him Jeshaiah of the sons of Merari, with his kinsmen and their sons, 20; besides 220 of the temple servants, whom David and his officials had set apart to attend the Levites. These were all mentioned by name.

Ezra has the king's permission to invite anyone to return to Jerusalem that wants to go. He gets them ready. He camps at the Ahava River. As he is chronicling who is going to go with him, he finds absolutely no one from the tribe of Levi. He is the only one. There are no other priests or Levites, the very people who lived off the offerings of the people in their designated cities and who were to tend to the temple and all of its responsibilities. They were to be the ones who instructed the people in the ways of God. What happened? Why did they not respond to the opportunity to return?

I don't know that we will ever know, but as a pastor I know how easy it is to get comfortable right where I am. I know how easy it is to explain this sort of move away and expect someone else to go. I also know it's easy to throw stones at people.

Ezra does not throw stones. He stays focused on solving the problem. He has a trip to take. He needs trusted spiritual leadership to join him. Instead of putting a guilt trip on everyone, he goes to one of the main leaders to gather some Levites for this move to Jerusalem. The result was that by God's hand, he was given a man of discretion, which means he was given a man who had the trait of judging wisely and objectively. Not only was he given Sherebiah, but he was also given his sons -- 18 in all. More than that, Ezra was given others like him as well.

What can you learn from this text that informs your fight? At the most basic level, you shouldn't fight alone. Don't go to the broken places alone. Don't respond to the onslaught you face alone. You need wisdom and objectivity around you. You need people who will take the journey with you, who will challenge you, sit with you, counsel with you and cry with you. This is one of the reasons we emphasize community groups as we do. We want people to connect with others to assist them in their Christian walk. We want people to know that they are not alone in whatever battle they are facing.

You see, every Ezra needs a Sherebiah. As a matter of fact, every Ezra needs many Sherebiahs because as Proverbs 24:6 declares, "For by wise guidance you can wage your war, and in abundance of counselors there is victory." That is Agape Development Ministries' story. That is ST-CHM's story and that is Pastor Petr's story as well. They all have others around them helping them take the ground they are burdened and called to take. To wage war, you need guidance.

Ezra knew he had a fight on his hands. He was called to teach the people the Word of God and challenge them to walk in His ways. Israel hadn't seen success in this in many years. He was a reformer. He knew that the road ahead was going to be tough. So, he surrounded himself with wise counsel. Then he called them to fast and pray.

REFLECTION QUESTIONS:

1. Describe the broken places of your fight? What does it look like?

2. What are the challenges you see? Where should you start in repairing and rebuilding?

3. Every Ezra needs a Sherebiah and every Moses needs Aaron and Hur. Who can you come alongside you to strengthen, give counsel and support?

CHAPTER 6

Fighting For Your Loved Ones: Placing Your Hand on God's Throne

Some of our most intense fights are for our children. Here is one mom's ongoing fight story as she battles for the hearts of her children.

My fight story is raising my children to love Jesus and to have a heart like His. When I was a mom of young children, our church's preschool, A Children's Village, ministered to our family like no one else. The administration, the teachers, and the moms displayed Jesus' love in all they did. From praying for my child's health, to invitations to coffee, to how the mom's served dinner to the teachers every year at teacher's appreciation dinner, I had never experienced anything like that. I wanted that in my life on a regular basis. In a few years time, my husband and I gave our lives to Christ in front of the congregation of West University Baptist Church.

Fast forward 18 years, our children are now teenagers. My
fight is to display the love and peace of Jesus in our home. It is
TOUGH! Much of the time teenage hormones, teenage wants,
and the desires of the world seem to be winning the heart and
attitude of my children. Not to mention the sin nature we all
struggle with! My husband and I are in a literal battle at home.
Conflict, raised voices, harsh words, confession, asking for forgiveness, consulting friends, pastors, and therapists – that seems
to be the cycle over and over again. But for the grace of God, we
are still standing. We are not giving up. Jesus gives us a new day
every day. As we continue to be in His Word daily, as we pray and
seek to be a faithful part of our church community, we know that
this is only temporary. Our children are God's. We continue to
pray for our adult children and their families and the love of Jesus
that will be displayed in their homes one day.

THERE'S NO OTHER FIGHT LIKE IT

When my kids pray their prayers as they go to bed, their most
frequent request is, "...and please keep me safe." You know, that's not
a bad prayer as some of our most basic prayers are prayers for protection. We see Jesus instruct us to pray this way in the Lord's Prayer
in Matthew 6:13, "...and lead us not into temptation, but deliver
us from evil." Jesus knew that one of our most fundamental needs,
if not the most fundamental need, was to feel safe. Ezra had a bold
faith and great belief in God's ability to protect. Some might call it a
foolish faith as he refused to ask for an escort to protect them on their
journey to Jerusalem.

> Then I proclaimed a fast there, at the river Ahava, that we
> might humble ourselves before our God, to seek from him a
> safe journey for ourselves, our children, and all our goods. For
> I was ashamed to ask the king for a band of soldiers and horse-
> men to protect us against the enemy on our way, since we had
> told the king, "The hand of our God is for good on all who seek
> him, and the power of his wrath is against all who forsake him."

So we fasted and implored our God for this, and he listened to our entreaty.

At the core of Ezra's life is the conviction that God was for them, and that He would provide for and protect them. Ezra most likely appeared before the king, made his request, and got the approval. The King probably said, "Now write up what we talked about, and I'll sign it for you." Ezra knew he was asking for a lot. He also knows that God was able to protect them. Once again, we see prayer and fasting. This time it is for protection.

As we talk about our fight stories, we must recognize that three forces wage war against us. It may intimidate you. But what we must understand is through the death and resurrection of Jesus, He conquered each enemy. Note the words of one of my favorite authors and theologians, Warren Wiersbe:

> As Christians, we face three enemies: the world, the flesh, and the devil (Eph. 2:1–3). "The world" refers to the system around us that is opposed to God, that caters to "the lust of the flesh, and the lust of the eyes, and the pride of life" (1 John 2:15–17). "Society apart from God" is a simple, but accurate, definition of "the world." "The flesh" is the old nature that we inherited from Adam, a nature that is opposed to God and can do nothing spiritual to please God. By His death and resurrection, Christ overcame the world (John 16:33; Gal. 6:14), and the flesh (Rom. 6:1–6; Gal. 2:20), and the devil (Eph. 1:19–23). In other words, as believers, we do not fight for victory—we fight from victory! The Spirit of God enables us, by faith, to appropriate Christ's victory for ourselves. [16]

I want to take you to another fight story called the battle at Rephidim. It's the Israelites first war as they moved through the wilderness after escaping the Egyptians. The Israelites encamped at Rephidim. They are thirsty. They are complaining. They ask Moses, "Did you bring us out here to die?" Moses asks the Lord what he should do, and the Lord tells him to take his staff and strike the rock. Moses does this, and the rock brings forth water.

Immediately following this action, the Israelites are attacked by their distant cousin, Amalek. The Amalekites bring war. Moses appoints Joshua to get some fighting men and go up against the Amalekites. The next day, Joshua gets these men and goes into the Valley of Rephidim, while Moses takes Aaron and Hur to the higher plain overlooking the valley. As we note what takes place on the higher plain with Moses, let's also note that someone had to go down to the valley and face the Amalekites. Though most of this chapter is going to be on putting our hand on the throne of God, we must also recognize the work that must take place. As this mom above notes, navigating the conversations, seeking out counsel from pastors and therapists, and doing the work necessary to be positioned to win is also a part of the fight we wage.

As the story unfolds, there is a back-and-forth battle. The results down in the valley correspond directly with the activity on the higher plain. Moses is holding his staff up high to the Lord. When his arms get weary and fall, the Amalekites advance. When he keeps his staff high, the Israelites advance. Ultimately, Aaron and Hur see this and hold up Moses' arms. Moses had the wisdom to bring others to the battle with him. These men were right there. They stood alongside Moses holding his arms up as together they interceded for Israel. The Israelites defeated the Amalekites.

> Then the LORD said to Moses, "Write this as a memorial in a book and recite it in the ears of Joshua, that I will utterly blot out the memory of Amalek from under heaven." And Moses built an altar and called the name of it, The LORD Is My Banner, 16 saying, "A hand upon the throne of the LORD! The LORD will have war with Amalek from generation to generation."

Do you see the declaration, "A hand upon the throne of the LORD!" As Moses builds the altar and declares, "The Lord is My Banner." But, what is he saying when he says, a hand upon the throne of the Lord? I believe he is saying:

- Had the battle not come…
- Had the friends not been there…
- Had he not gone to the high plain to intercede…
- Had he not held high the staff of God…

HE NEVER WOULD HAVE EXPERIENCED THE SWEETNESS OF THIS VICTORY WHERE HE TOUCHED THE THRONE OF GOD!

To fight the battle in prayer is to touch the throne of God and come out victorious. You see, enduring the fight creates a sweetness in our relationships with Christ. This is the irreplaceable fellowship that we can only get because He gets us through the battle to the other side.

Ephesians 6:10-20 instructs us with these words:

> Finally, be strong in the Lord and in the strength of his might. Put on the whole armor of God, that you may be able to stand against the schemes of the devil. For we do not wrestle against flesh and blood, but against the rulers, against the authorities, against the cosmic powers over this present darkness, against the spiritual forces of evil in the heavenly places. Therefore take up the whole armor of God, that you may be able to withstand in the evil day, and having done all, to stand firm. Stand therefore, having fastened on the belt of truth, and having put on the breastplate of righteousness, and, as shoes for your feet, having put on the readiness given by the gospel of peace. In all circumstances take up the shield of faith, with which you can extinguish all the flaming darts of the evil one; and take the helmet of salvation, and the sword of the Spirit, which is the word of God, praying at all times in the Spirit, with all prayer and supplication. To that end keep alert with all perseverance, making supplication for all the saints, and also for me, that words may be given to me in opening my mouth boldly to proclaim the mystery of the gospel, for which I am an ambassador in chains, that I may declare it boldly, as I ought to speak.

During World War II, an officer was briefing his men on how to take a certain objective. He demonstrated to them the manner in which they needed to hug the ground so as to stay below enemy fire. He said in conclusion, "If you advance on your knees, you will always be safe."

HOW DO WE ADVANCE OUR FIGHT ON OUR KNEES?

Mark Batterson, in his book, The Circle Maker Prayer Journal, wrote:

"Spiritual battles are always won or lost on your knees...(for) God loves it when you fight for him, but He loves it even more when you let Him fight for you."

Ephesians 6:18a tells us, "...praying at all times in the Spirit, with all prayer and supplication." Prayer is the energy that we need to engage in the spiritual battle. In prayer is the sweetness and intimacy to carry us through the fight as we put a hand on the throne of God.

To advance on our knees, we must:

• Pray always
• Pray in the Spirit
• Pray with all prayer and supplication

Pray Always

What does it mean to pray always? Does this mean that we are to pray 24/7 – never sleeping or never working? To pray always seems very intimidating, especially when you already know that you don't pray enough.

The words here literally mean, "in every season," or "on every occasion." In other words, there is nothing that passes through our lives that we shouldn't be submitting to the Lord in prayer. This is a good starting point. This is reinforced in Romans 12:12 with the words, "... be constant in prayer," and 1 Thessalonians 5:17, with the call to, "... pray without ceasing."

This morning, at the time of this writing, I took my daughter Carson to her first day of Spirit Camp at her school. She made the middle school spirit squad that includes cheerleading and dance and their first practice is today. She expressed some nerves and a bit of unease to her mom last evening. They talked through it and Julee gave her some great pointers. Today, as I drove her to her school, I didn't bring up the nerves. Instead, I said, "Hey, let's pray for your camp today. You go first." As Carson started to pray, she brought up her nerves and her excitement. I then prayed for her and asked God to both protect her and give her favor as she puts herself out there as a cheerleader.

Did you know that nothing is too small for you to take to your gracious Heavenly Father? We are to pray in every season and on every occasion—even those days when we start cheer camp.

As Paul instructs us on the spiritual battle, we learn that the context is oppression. Paul describes it as the "day of evil." The enduring energy that we need for the battle is found in prayer. Praying always is a call to persist and persevere in prayer.

It is the picture of Moses persisting to hold his staff high. That staff represented his calling to go to Egypt; the power of God to move Pharoah's heart; God's deliverance by parting the waters of the Red Sea; and God's provision to meet their needs, as Moses had just used it to bring water forth from a rock.

When Moses went to the high plain while Joshua was fighting down in the valley, Moses held his staff high. It is as if he is saying:

"God, all I can do is submit this to you. Here it is. Take it. I hold it up to you. All you have called me to, all that we have been through, all that you have provided, I submit it to you. I am powerless to do anything. I am powerless to bring about victory. God, here it is. If we are going to win, it is because you bring about the victory!"

Because Moses had Aaron and Hur with him, he was able to persist in prayer, lifting his hands to the heavens. As he tired, his hands fell. But because he was not alone, they propped his hands up, held them high, and together, they persisted.

Are you persisting in prayer? Are you continuing to cry out to God in the midst of the oppression? Are you on your knees? Are you letting others join you as you tire?

Pray in the Spirit

The second way we are to pray in the midst of the fight is by praying in the Spirit, which means we are to pray submitted unto the Holy Spirit. Two key passages in Ephesians speak of the Holy Spirit's role in our lives to empower us and fill us. Ephesians 3:16 says, "…that according to the riches of his glory he may grant you to be strengthened with power through his Spirit in your inner being…"

The Holy Spirit gives us the power to endure, the power to keep going, and the power to respond to the day of evil, as Christ would respond. The Holy Spirit gives power for us to live life as Christ lived it. Remember, prayer is the place where we receive energy for the battle. The Holy Spirit gives us the counsel to walk as God would have us walk. He speaks God's word into our lives that we might speak it out as we use the sword of the Spirit.

As you continue to read Ephesians 3, you see the impact of being submitted to the Holy Spirit. Ephesians 3:17-20 states:

> so that Christ may dwell in your hearts through faith—that you, being rooted and grounded in love, may have strength to comprehend with all the saints what is the breadth and length and height and depth, and to know the love of Christ that surpasses knowledge, that you may be filled with all the fullness of God.

As we pray in the Spirit, submitted unto Him, Christ dwells in our hearts. We are rooted and established in love – helping us to stand firm. We get a greater understanding, along with all the saints of God, of His love and His work on our behalf. We know Christ's love more intimately. We are filled with the fullness of God. All of this is available to us during the evil day.

Then, when the trial passes and the enemy flees, and you have remained standing firm, you have a sweetness and intimacy with Christ because your hand has touched the throne of God.

We are also commanded in Ephesians 5:18 to be filled with the Spirit. It says:

> And do not get drunk with wine, for that is debauchery, but be filled with the Spirit…

When we pray in the Spirit, we simply ask God to fill us. My simple prayer is this, "Lord, fill me with your Spirit, I pray." As I make final preparations to preach, I pray, "Lord fill me up that you might pour me out." We can't give out what we don't have. But to have the Spirit comfortable and at home in our hearts, we must turn aside from the things of the world. In this passage, the call is to not be controlled by alcohol. That is what drunkenness is. It's a call to be controlled by the Holy Spirit. To pray in the Spirit, to be filled with the Spirit, and it is to be controlled by the Spirit because we are submitted to the Holy Spirit.

This simple prayer says, "Lord, I submit myself to you and turn from the things of the world." When we do this, there is a sweetness that comes. There is an intimacy and appreciation that comes to us.

Notice it in the rest of this portion in Ephesians 5:18-21.

> And do not get drunk with wine, for that is debauchery, but be filled with the Spirit, addressing one another in psalms and hymns and spiritual songs, singing and making melody to the Lord with your heart, giving thanks always and for everything to

God the Father in the name of our Lord Jesus Christ, submitting to one another out of reverence for Christ.

Notice how when we are submitted to the Holy Spirit and filled with the Holy Spirit, there is a love for God and others that flows out of our lives. Notice the phrasing:

- Addressing one another

- Singing to the Lord with our hearts

- Giving thanks to God the Father

- Submitting to one another

The first and the fourth phrases speak of our horizontal relationships to one another. The second and third phrases speak of our vertical relationship to the Father.

I can't help but think of Aaron and Hur on that high plain with Moses. Moses knew he needed his brothers with him. Moses knew that the fight was too vast to stand up there alone. Moses had Aaron and Hur join him on that high plain. They gladly did. They held up his arms. They devised a plan. They propped up his arms with a rock. They stood in the gap with him in intercession in the midst of that fight. I bet their relationship was never the same.

My friend and former colleague, Jennifer Dean said of this passage:

> "When I look at these Bible stories, I try to put myself into the story. Who do I relate to and how does that affect me? In this case, the truth is at some point in my life, I will be in every one of these positions.
>
> I might be in the valley, unsure of what is going on, fighting for my life and looking up to those I can trust to intercede for me, to be an example to me. I may be close to someone who is going

through a hard battle and they need me to stand with them and hold up their arms to help get them through.

I may be the one, desperately calling out to God and in need of others to come around and support me in the battle. Being in the fight and being the one who is interceding to God are two of the most difficult seasons to walk through, but two of the sweetest results because you experience God in a way you never could, had you not walked through that battle."

Pray in the Spirit, for to fight the battle in prayer, is to touch the throne of God and come out victorious.

Pray with All Prayer and Supplication

This last phrase of Ephesians 6:18 says, "…with all prayer and supplication." What does it mean to pray with all prayer and supplication?

A lot of people, when they pray, view it as asking God for stuff. Some people even say, "Oh, I don't want to be a bother to God. I only ask God for the big things that are taking place in my life." But, many people do not pray, because they believe that God is limited and if his resources get used up on them, then someone else in need won't get resources used on their "greater needs."

This is a poverty mindset when it comes to prayer. It is the mindset that God only has so many blessings that He can dole out. But God is the God of abundance. He is not bound. There is no poverty in Him.

With that said, prayer certainly is asking God for His intervention. When you see or hear the word supplication, I want you to think, "Heaping and Keeping." The word, "supplication," means an imploring request for blessings or the aversion of evils that we fear. So, we are to pray in a manner that asks the Father to heap his blessings on us and keep evils off us.

Keeping Prayer: One of the things that I pray over my children when we are saying our prayers together is that God would keep disease and evil far from them.

Heaping Prayer: I also pray that God would bestow His favor and blessings upon them – in the classroom, in the hallways, with friends, and on the athletic fields.

Consider supplication in the fight in which you find yourself. This would be a prayer that says something like this:

> *"Lord, would you keep the advances of the enemy off me? Would you establish me? Lord, would you thwart the plan of the enemy? And Father, would you heap your blessings upon me as I seek to do your will? Would you bless me in a way that not only I know you did this, but that others see you are at work on my behalf? Father, glorify your name through this!"*

That's supplication – keeping and heaping! I am sure so much of Ezra's prayer as they began that journey was a prayer of supplication, asking the Lord to keep the evil away and heap His blessings upon them.

What about praying with all prayer? This includes prayer that isn't just requests of heaping and keeping.

Consider other forms of prayer:

- **Confession:** This is the asking for forgiveness and cleansing of sin. Sometimes we sin and invite the enemy in to get a foothold on our hearts and lives. We must regularly search our hearts and ask for God's forgiveness and cleansing.

- **Praise and Thanksgiving:**
  Warren Wiersbe says, "Thanksgiving is a great prayer weapon for defeating Satan. Praise changes things."
  Mark Batterson says, "Whatever you don't turn into praise turns into pride."

So, we need to pray prayers of praise and thanksgiving.

- **Intercession:** Praying on behalf of others.

- **Prayers for our Enemies:** Listen to Jesus' words in Matthew 5:43-44. It says, "You have heard that it was said, 'You shall love your neighbor and hate your enemy.' But I say to you, Love your enemies and pray for those who persecute you…"

Praying for your enemy is hard and sometimes I have found myself doing so with my jaw clenched. The only reason I did it was out of obedience. But when I pray for my enemy, I am agreeing with the Scripture in Ephesians 6 that says, "Our battle is not against flesh and blood, but against rulers, and authorities and principalities in the heavenly realm."

When I pray for my enemy, I pray that God would bless them to repentance. I pray that through this exchange that God would use me to reveal the Lord to them. It not an easy prayer, but it is one where we touch the throne of God.

MY PRAYER FOR YOU

> *I pray that you know that when the battle comes, there is a depth, sweetness, and intimacy that you are going to develop with Christ and with those you ask to journey with you that can only come because you put your hand on his throne. Pray always. Pray in the Spirit and pray with all prayer and supplication! May God keep you and heap upon you His many blessings available to you in Christ Jesus!*

REFLECTION QUESTIONS:

1. Nothing passes through our lives that we shouldn't be submitting to the Lord in prayer. Is this your posture? If so, what have been the benefits of being constant in prayer? If not, what is happening in your life right now that you haven't put before our Lord in prayer?

2. Prayer is the place where we receive the energy we need for the battles we face. Are you praying to be filled and empowered by the Spirit? Circle the simple prayers you feel you need to consistently pray:

- "Lord, I submit myself to you and turn from the things of the world."
- "Lord, fill me with your Spirit, I pray."
- Prayers of Confession
- Prayers of Intercession
- Prayers of Praise and Thanksgiving

3. Before you move to the next chapter, would you pray this prayer of supplication – a keeping and heaping prayer?

"Lord, would you keep the advances of the enemy off me? Would you establish me? Lord, would you thwart the plan of the enemy? And Father, would you heap your blessings upon me as I seek to do your will? Would you bless me in a way that not only I know you did this, but that others see you are at work on my behalf? Father, glorify your name through this!"

SECTION 3

Fighting For Your Church: Be a Builder

Ezra 2:68-70 states:

> Some of the heads of families, when they came to the house of the Lord that is in Jerusalem, made freewill offerings for the house of God, to erect it on its site. According to their ability they gave to the treasury of the work 61,000 darics of gold, 5,000 minas of silver, and 100 priests' garments.

> Now the priests, the Levites, some of the people, the singers, the gatekeepers, and the temple servants lived in their towns, and all the rest of Israel in their towns.

Can you imagine what that first ascent to the city of Jerusalem must have felt like? Traditionally, the road from Jericho to Jerusalem would have been the pathway. This road was a 17-mile switchback that went roughly from 800 feet below sea-level to about 2500 feet above sea-level.

I can imagine that first glimpse of the temple mount, where the people have journeyed through the shattered walls and gates of this once amazing, fortified city. I can see the tears streaming down their faces and hear the hush of the crowd as they inch nearer and nearer to the site of the once great temple that now lie in ruins.

Oh, the weight that must have been on the shoulders of those leaders! Can you imagine the people rumbling to one another, "Are we really going to rebuild the temple? Oh, it's so much worse that I imagined!" Others may have said, "Why are we here? Should we really have left our homes in Babylon?"

Why has God stirred in the heart of Cyrus to allow the temple to be rebuilt in the city of Jerusalem? Why, today, are we working so hard to re-gather and rebuild the church after this season of separation?

In a sentence, it's all for the glory of God.

John Piper, in his classic work, Let the Nations Be Glad, opens this book with these words:

> "Missions is not the ultimate goal of the church. Worship is. Missions exists because worship doesn't. Worship is ultimate, not missions, because God is ultimate, not man. When this age is over, and the countless millions of the redeemed fall on their faces before the throne of God, missions will be no more. It is a temporary necessity. But worship abides forever." [17]

If you know anything about John Piper and his ministry, you may be familiar with the term "Christian Hedonism," meaning the call of believers in Jesus Christ to delight in God and enjoy him forever. This call to be glad in God comes from a "white-hot enjoyment of God's glory."[18]

Psalm 67:3-4 declares,

> Let the peoples praise you, O God;
> let all the peoples praise you!
> Let the nations be glad and sing for joy,
> for you judge the peoples with equity
> and guide the nations upon earth.

Throughout the Bible, the glory of God is front and center. The purpose of being created, chosen, and called is for the glory of God. Consider these verses on the glory of God and his purposes here on earth. [19]

> Isaiah 43:6-7 – God has created us for His glory:
> I will say to the north, Give up,
> and to the south, Do not withhold;
> bring my sons from afar
> and my daughters from the end of the earth,
> everyone who is called by my name,
> whom I created for my glory,
> whom I formed and made."

> Isaiah 49:3 – God's call of Israel is for His glory:
> And he said to me, "You are my servant,
> Israel, in whom I will be glorified."

Ephesians 1:4-6 – God chose the church for His glory:

> …even as he chose us in him before the foundation of the world, that we should be holy and blameless before him. In love he predestined us for adoption to himself as sons through Jesus Christ, according to the purpose of his will, to the praise of his glorious grace, with which he has blessed us in the Beloved.

Ezekiel 36:22-23 – God restored Israel from exile for His glorious name:

"Therefore say to the house of Israel, Thus says the Lord God: It is not for your sake, O house of Israel, that I am about to act, but for the sake of my holy name, which you have profaned among the nations to which you came. And I will vindicate the holiness of my great name, which has been profaned among the nations, and which you have profaned among them. And the nations will know that I am the Lord, declares the Lord God, when through you I vindicate my holiness before their eyes.

As the second chapter of Ezra closes, the author reveals that the group coming out of exile are on a mission – to re-establish the altar and to begin the process of rebuilding the temple to fight for the glory of God in Jerusalem.

CHAPTER 7

Fighting for Glory: Worship Fuels the Fight

I have had the rich privilege of serving alongside Pastor Chuck Oak on our executive pastoral staff. Chuck has been all over the world leading teams of people to deploy their influence for the purpose and glory of God. He knows what it is to fight for the glory of God and for the health of the local church. Chuck went through a very difficult season many years ago as the church he served nearly split. By the grace of God, he and his colleagues were able to help this congregation heal and move forward. Look at his fight story as he fought for his church.

While serving on the pastor's executive staff at a large church in Northeast Houston, I and my three other colleagues experienced firsthand the evil of Satan and his long-term desire to bring down the Lord's church. The church was taking lots of new ground for the kingdom when an attitude of discontentment with the senior pastor began to emerge. This stemmed from a number of issues with the pastor. The four of us concluded that he had not violated any moral or civil law; therefore, we decided to honor the office of the pastor. If God wanted him gone, He certainly could accomplish that.

The pastor eventually did resign. That's when things really turned south for us four. Those who wanted him out were incensed that we didn't push him out. Those who wanted him to stay were angry that we did not support him by attempting to make him rethink his decision. That's when we bonded. We committed to each other we would not leave this fight for another church. We will stay; we will pray; we will trust God. That's when it got worse.

I was tasked to answer e-mails from a special account for people to ask any questions. It was open season for venom deposits. My wife writes in her book, "I often came home from work to find him on the living room sofa, curled up in the fetal position. He had stopped functioning. He gave everything he had at the office, fighting for the struggling church."

Well, the Lord moved in a miraculous way. I believe it was by faith, by prayers, and by singing praises to the One on the throne, where God broke all of us. We ordered several pallets of bricks and built a wall in front of the stage which went the entire length of the stage. During the invitation we invited people to come, take a brick, and help us symbolically tear down the wall we had built between the two sides. One by one they came. It was one of the most amazing scenes of forgiveness, repentance, and tears of acceptance I have ever witnessed. Nehemiah worked to restore the wall, but sometimes you must tear down the old one so He can build something new.

Was it worth it? The fight? The hurt? Oh yes! It began to be a happy place again. The word spread. People who had left returned. The budget was restored. The baptismal waters were active. By the time the new pastor was called, the church was poised to explode. At its lowest point there were about 1,100 in attendance. Today, the building has been remodeled and expanded and over 3,000 are in worship to the glory of God. They continue to take new ground. And for me, when I return for a funeral or special occasion, I'm affectionately known as one of the four horsemen of the apocalypse. Only God could do that!

What is the church to you? Is it a place for Sunday worship? Is it a place of friendship and fellowship? Is it a place to use your gifts and serve your fellow believer? Is it the place where you are challenged to grow in your faith and have your character cultivated? Is it the place where you connect with God?

The simple answer to each of these questions is yes. The church is a place to gather to worship, to fellowship, to serve, and to be challenged. It is a place where infants in the faith can come and grow into strong young men and women, who become strengthened to overcome. It's the place where mature men and women in the faith can act as parents to help the young grow so they too can become spiritual parents. It is a place to connect with God and with fellow believers.

The church is the place where the Word of God is proclaimed and where the people of God gather to be built up in order to be sent out. The church is described as the body of Christ and the bride of Christ. It's the gathering of the called-out ones. It is what Jesus said that He would build, and the gates of hell would not conquer. We know all of these things about the church. But what if we understood the church to be the gathering point to be fueled up and filled up for the fight of our lives? What if it became the place where we pulled in, opened up the gas tank and made sure the fuel line was inserted so that we could be prepared for the road ahead as we live for the glory of God?

NEW BEGINNINGS

As we step into Ezra chapter three, the first corporate worship gathering of this post-exilic people takes place at the temple site.

Here, they will rebuild the altar of God and make offerings as required by the law. Ezra 3:1-7 states:

> When the seventh month came, and the children of Israel were in the towns, the people gathered as one man to Jerusalem. Then arose Jeshua the son of Jozadak, with his fellow priests, and Zerubbabel the son of Shealtiel with his kinsmen, and they built the altar of the God of Israel, to offer burnt offerings on it, as it is written in the Law of Moses the man of God. They set the altar in its place, for fear was on them because of the peoples of the lands, and they offered burnt offerings on it to the Lord, burnt offerings morning and evening. And they kept the Feast of Booths, as it is written, and offered the daily burnt offerings by number according to the rule, as each day required, and after that the regular burnt offerings, the offerings at the new moon and at all the appointed feasts of the Lord, and the offerings of everyone who made a freewill offering to the Lord. From the first day of the seventh month they began to offer burnt offerings to the Lord. But the foundation of the temple of the Lord was not yet laid. So they gave money to the masons and the carpenters, and food, drink, and oil to the Sidonians and the Tyrians to bring cedar trees from Lebanon to the sea, to Joppa, according to the grant that they had from Cyrus king of Persia.

This first day of the seventh month marked a new beginning for Judah. On the last Sunday of February of 1928, a new beginning called West University Baptist Church also took place as a small gathering of people assembled on the front porch of Nannie B. David's home. Miss David had retired from the Foreign Mission Board of the Southern Baptist Convention, after a career as a nurse missionary in Africa. Now, she was settling into the old rice fields that was a developing bedroom community west of Rice University. Nannie David was herself a pioneer – a woman in the 1920's starting a church! But she was just doing what the people of God do when they come to a community where there is no church present: establishing a gospel witness that would bring glory to God for generations.

New beginnings come in all shapes and sizes, don't they? I remember the day Justo Robinson emailed me about meeting together. I first met Pastor Justo in 1992 when I was 20 years old. He was the pastor of the "Spanish Mission" of First Baptist Church of Missouri City, Texas. Justo taught school with my wife's father, Jim King. To this day, they still have a great respect for one another.

In the fall of 2014, Pastor Justo asked if we can meet. I had not seen Pastor Justo for many years, but I was glad to meet with him and see how he was doing. When Justo came to my office, we grabbed a cup of coffee, caught up a bit, and then he said, "Roger, God has placed your name on my heart at least two times. Both times, I was in the sanctuary. I was in prayer, asking the Lord to show me what He wanted to do at the church." He explained to me how all of the English-speaking congregants had either died or moved on. He and his church had been walking by faith for many years. He believed that the Lord had so much more for them. As a church, they had more property than they could steward well for the size of the congregation. His heart's cry was for God to be glorified once again at this campus. He said something like, "I think the Lord wants me to see if you all will make this a campus of your congregation."

I immediately felt the weight of these words. This was the old First Baptist Church of Missouri City, now called Emmanuel Baptist Church. It was the place where my wife grew up and responded to the gospel call on her life. It was where she was baptized and where so much of her early discipleship took place.

It was also the church where I was pulled back into the body of Christ. As a teen, we had a bad experience at the church where I grew up. In many ways, I was spiritually adrift. I wasn't anchored. I wasn't worshipping. I wasn't seeking God. But God was seeking me.

During the summer before my sophomore year of college, I was invited to a Bible study that met on Tuesday nights, by a friend at my work. That Bible study was at the home of Jim and Brenda King, and it was the Bible study of the college ministry of First Baptist Missouri

City. Through that invitation, I met my wife, Julee, their daughter, and I have never been the same. Don't you know that I quickly joined that church?

I got plugged in once again to the body of Christ. It was on a retreat through this church's college ministry that I was called to ministry. This church was where I preached my first sermon and was licensed to the gospel ministry. As you can imagine, it had a significant tug on my heart.

I'm humbled by writing this story. I wonder how many other stories like this God is going to tell. As I write this in summer 2021, our local Baptist association here in Houston is working with nine churches on the brink of closing their doors. Thom Rainer, former CEO of Lifeway Christian Resources once said that he believed there were about 10,000 churches a year on the brink of closure for the foreseeable future. Some of these churches will sell their property to a grocer or some other developer. Others will limp along, selling off parcel by parcel. Others will seek to revitalize while others, like Emmanuel Baptist in Missouri City, will proactively seek the right partner to replant and find a new beginning.

A pastor I deeply respected was now sitting in my office saying, "We need the right partner to fully steward all that God has given to us." He was asking for my help and our church's involvement as he sought a new beginning for the house of God at 2106 5th Street in Missouri City, Texas. He was believing God for more glory!

STAYING TRUE IN A HOSTILE ENVIRONMENT

I want to publicly commend Pastor Justo for his willingness to keep fighting for God's glory and God's plan on God's timeline. He told me a few stories of how different people wanted to come along-side and move their church into his. He told me of one pastor from Oklahoma who showed up and sat through a few Sunday services. The pastor said, "As I sought to find out who this guy was, he had the audacity to say to me, 'I'm trying to figure out if this is where I am going to move my congregation.'"

Justo was given good opportunities, but he sensed they weren't what the Lord wanted. After sitting with me, we began to walk together. But no one was in a hurry. As a matter of fact, it wasn't until 2020 that his congregation dissolved and became a part of our church family.

As the story of the temple rebuild begins, one of the things that we notice in Ezra 3 is that when the altar is rebuilt, it is put back in its original spot. Ezra 3:2b-3 says:

> "…and they built the altar of the God of Israel, to offer burnt offerings on it, as it is written in the Law of Moses the man of God. They set the altar in its place, for fear was on them because of the peoples of the lands, and they offered burnt offerings on it to the Lord, burnt offerings morning and evening."

There are two things worthy of noting here. First, Joshua, the High Priest, and the leaders with him were committed to the Word of God. As they rebuilt the altar, they were doing so as prescribed in the Law of Moses. This is so vital, if we are going to fight for the glory of God. God's word is eternal and powerful and is given to accomplish God's work. Churches that move away from the Word of God because of liberal theology deteriorate over time.

The second thing is that as they set the altar in its place, they were fearful because of the peoples of the lands. These were people from Ashdod, Samaria, Ammon, Moab, and Edom,[20] who created all sorts of challenges along the way. M. Brenamen notes:

> The Jewish community determined to worship God according to the ancient specifications, and the emphasis on continuity persist-ed. They built the altar "on its foundation," which no doubt means on its exact preexilic location. In the Old Testament, building an altar was a significant act. In the life of the patriarchs, it marked a new dedication to God or a new experience of God's presence and

leading... "Burnt offerings" also emphasized dedication, consecration, and commitment; in the burnt offerings the whole animal
was burned as a symbol of total consecration to God. [21]

This is such an important point to make. Zerubbabel, Joshua,
and the entire team are fully committed to this plan. There is a total
consecration to God! I can only imagine that when they and the
50,000 Jews with them rolled back into town, the pressures began
to mount. These pressures were expressed in intimidation, in threats,
and in the temptation to shift beliefs to better fit into their culture.
This is not unlike the pressure that the culture is putting on us today
– pressure to conform to their views of sexuality and gender. It's
called syncretism. Isn't it fascinating that thousands of years later,
the prince of this world is still running the same old plays of intimidation and fear? Or, if he senses a weakness, he tempts with the al-
lurement of better, more relevant tomorrows if you just compromise
what you believe today.

Remember, the Jews have the permission of Cyrus, the King of
Persia, to build the temple on this site. But we must also realize that
Cyrus and his main officials are a long way away. The Jews have been
granted this, but that doesn't mean the people that were being displaced were happy about it. Their presence created fear in the hearts
of the Jews, but the Jews courageously moved forward to build back
the altar and offer sacrifices. It was a new beginning!

STRENGTH IN NUMBERS

Courage comes when, "…the people gathered as one man to
Jerusalem" (Ezra 3:1). This was one of the ways they battled their
fears. Gathering for worship demonstrates a strong sense of community and common bond of faith in God. In celebrating the Feast
of Booths despite the opposition and danger, they showed faith to
move ahead. They choose to live in tents for seven days to
commemorate the 40 years of wandering in the wilderness. The fear
was palpable. But gathering in worship helps us deal with difficult
and even dangerous situations.

I remember the first Sunday back amid the COVID-19 Pandemic, when we opened back up for on-campus worship. We made the conscious decision to provide both on-campus and on-line worship, enabling the attenders, in a spirit of liberty, to decide how they would gather corporately with us. On May 31, 2021, in a socially distanced sanctuary with no more than 60 people as we sang songs of praise, I felt like I was getting to take a drink of water for the first time in a long time. Gathering with others and singing out to the Lord refreshed my soul. I left thinking, "Okay, we can do this."

Corporate worship is vital to our lives, to our homes and to our communities. When we gather where the Bible is preached, and the songs of the faith are sung, we hear of the majesty, glory, and holiness of God. We read the Word and hear it proclaimed to us. We hear of mankind's rebellion, the love of God to give us a Savior, and the need for us to submit to the Lord Jesus Christ. We hear the truth that we are to be his ambassadors. We are to take the gospel across the street and around the world. We need this revelation into our lives on a weekly basis. As Proverbs 29:18a proclaims, "Where there is no prophetic vision the people cast off restraint."

THE IMPORTANCE OF PREACHING

As you read the entirety of Ezra and Nehemiah, Ezra, the scribe and priest, plays a prominent role in the Word of God being proclaimed to the people of God. As we saw previously, Ezra is skilled in the Law. He has set his heart to both observe it and help others know it as well. God uses Ezra as the people gather congregationally for a tremendous renewal. Nehemiah 8:1-3 states:

> And all the people gathered as one man into the square before the Water Gate. And they told Ezra the scribe to bring the Book of the Law of Moses that the Lord had commanded Israel. So Ezra the priest brought the Law before the assembly, both men and women and all who could understand what they heard, on the first day of the seventh month. And he read from it facing the square before the Water Gate from early morning until midday,

in the presence of the men and the women and those who could understand. And the ears of all the people were attentive to the Book of the Law.

Why does God use the preaching of the Scripture to grow our lives? I believe it enables us to live a life for His glory -- one that is abounding with the wisdom and knowledge of God. As the Apostle Paul said in Romans 10:17, "So faith comes from hearing, and hearing through the word of Christ."

When we submit ourselves to the revelation of God, it informs our way. Psalm 119:105 says, "Your word is a lamp to my feet and a light to my path." We need the Word revealed to us to enlighten our hearts and inform our way, because as we already saw, where there is no revelation from God, people cast off restraint.

PAUL'S PRAYER FOR THE CHURCH

In Ephesians, the Apostle Paul prays a significant prayer for the church.

> For this reason, because I have heard of your faith in the Lord Jesus and your love toward all the saints, I do not cease to give thanks for you, remembering you in my prayers, that the God of our Lord Jesus Christ, the Father of glory, may give you the Spirit of wisdom and of revelation in the knowledge of him, having the eyes of your hearts enlightened, that you may know what is the hope to which he has called you, what are the riches of his glorious inheritance in the saints, and what is the immeasurable greatness of his power toward us who believe, according to the working of his great might that he worked in Christ when he raised him from the dead and seated him at his right hand in the heavenly places, far above all rule and authority and power and dominion, and above every name that is named, not only in this age but also in the one to come. And he put all things under his feet and gave

him as head over all things to the church, which is his body, the fullness of him who fills all in all. (Ephesians 1:15-23)

In the ancient world, the city of Ephesus was a place of knowledge. It was a city known as a place of learning, and it attracted a concentration of scholars to its lecture halls to speak on various subjects. In fact, in Acts 19, after Paul landed in Ephesus, he didn't get much traction preaching to the Jews in the synagogue, so he moved on to a lecture hall called the Hall of Tyrannus. For two years, he preached the gospel there to both Jews and Gentiles. Public lectures were given in places like the Hall of Odeum, which seated about 1,000 people, to promote knowledge and learning.

In this context Paul tells the Ephesian church that he wants them to increase in knowledge. This was his heart and prayer for them. He says, "For this reason…" In other words, because you've been given every spiritual blessing and because of your faith in Jesus and your love for the saints, here is my prayer for you:

Look at the content of Paul's prayer in verses 17 and 18.

…that the God of our Lord Jesus Christ, the Father of glory, may give you the Spirit of wisdom and of revelation in the knowledge of him, 18 having the eyes of your hearts enlightened, that you may know…

Paul is praying for believers to have more knowledge of God. You see, when we have a greater knowledge of God, our hearts burn to serve him. John Piper says:

God is the absolute reality that everyone in the universe must come to terms with. Everything depends utterly on his will. All other realities compare to him like a raindrop compares to the ocean or like an anthill compares to Mount Everest. To ignore him or belittle him is unintelligible and suicidal folly. How shall one ever be the emissary of this great God who has not trembled before him with joyful wonder?[22]

God's church must be filled with God's knowledge! But the question is what kind of knowledge? There is a difference between the true knowledge Paul is talking about and knowledge for knowledge's sake.

Here in Houston, Texas, I live in a city, that is full of knowledge—Rice University, the Texas Medical Center, and the University of Houston. Houston is also the energy capital of the world. Our city is full of knowledge. We live in a country and world that is full of knowledge. In fact, knowledge and information is increasing at a rapid pace.

Architect and futurist, Buckminster Fuller, promoted his theory called the "Knowledge Doubling Curve," which says that until 1900, human knowledge doubled about every century. By the end of World War II, it was doubling every 25 years. At the time of the publication of his book in the 1980s, Fuller proclaimed that knowledge was doubling every 12-13 months. IBM later added that by 2020, the internet of things would double knowledge every 12 or so hours. This led one writer to declare that the lifespan of the knowledge we have is shorter, thus we need to both learn and unlearn many things.[23]

I am not saying that there's anything wrong with increasing in knowledge. God gave us brilliant minds to think, create, and solve problems in the world. But, when it comes to knowledge in the church and our faith, there are at least three problems that will probably touch us all:

1. **Lack of Knowledge**—The church has a lack of knowledge when it comes to the Bible, theology, and truth. In an age of post-modernity and relativism, we must know the sound doctrines of our faith. Like Ezra, we must be skilled in the Word of the Lord so as to withstand the pressures to conform.

2. **False knowledge**—Some people know a lot, but do they know the right things? Consider the Jehovah's Witnesses. They knock on the door and want to share their gospel and seek to convert people to their beliefs. They have been schooled and trained in their doctrine, but it's a doctrine that doesn't hold to the etenality and deity of

Christ. They know lots of teaching and seem to have a very good heart. They have knowledge and zeal, but they have missed the way with a core tenant, non-negotiable to orthodox Christianity.

3. **True knowledge vs. Information**—Information is possessing knowledge for the sake of knowledge, as some have made knowing God a cerebral thing. They know all the right theories and arguments, but they don't live out what they know. This knowledge puffs up. With people like this, love is the thing that is missing. It's the difference of knowing about God through information obtained on a YouTube video, a website, or even a theology class, and truly knowing God personally.

Paul says, "I pray that God will give you a Spirit of wisdom and revelation in the knowledge of him…" The word knowledge is from a Greek word that means to make contact with; to know first-hand. God's intention is that He would continually reveal more and more of Himself to us. Paul calls God, the "glorious Father of our Lord Jesus Christ." Another translation says, "Father of Glory."

Glory, in the Scripture, refers to what makes God visible, or to His activity of making visible. God is a God whose nature is to reveal Himself. Thus, He is called, "The Father of Glory." He delights in receiving glory from his creation. As His gathered people, we must grasp His desire to reveal His glory through the church.

Consider the three things that Paul prays for the church. He prays that the church would know:

- The hope of our calling (v. 18a)
- The riches of our inheritance (v. 18b)
- The greatness of His power (v. 19)

Request #1: To Know the Hope of our Calling

Ephesians 1:18b says, "… that you may know what is the hope to which he has called you…"

The word "calling" is important in the Bible. The word for church means those who are "called out." We are told in 1 Peter 2:9 that we are, "…called out of darkness into His marvelous light." Later in the book, Paul says, "There is one body and one Spirit—just as you were called to the one hope that belongs to your call…" (Eph. 4:4).

Because we are "called out by God," we are to take "hope" in that truth. Not in the sense of "I hope so" but in the sense of "assurance for the future." Hope is assurance of the future with present implications!

This is what is so important about hope:

- We have the hope of Christ's return for His bride, the church.

- We have the hope of resurrection.

- We have the hope of heaven.

We have a certainty of the future with present implications. We have been called to be children of God. We have been called to live in obedience to Christ. We have been called to participate in his eternal glory. We have been called to give Him glory now and to share with those in our lives and beyond of this glorious God we serve.

But, Peter tells us that even though those things are in the future, we were, "born again into a living hope," that encourages us to live for Christ each and every day. 1 Peter 2:9 states:

> But you are not like that, for you are a chosen people. You are royal priests, a holy nation, God's very own possession. As a result, you can show others the goodness of God, for he called you out of the darkness into his wonderful light.

As we live today, in light of that calling, we can show others the goodness of God and this brings God glory. Warren Wiersbe says:

"The hope that belongs to our calling should be a dynamic force in our lives, encouraging us to be pure, obedient, and faithful. The fact that we shall one day see Christ and be like Him should motivate us to live like Christ today."

Do you know that hope to which you have been called? Are you in Christ? If so, you have been chosen as his son or daughter to be joint heirs with Christ. Your future is secure. Live today in light of that security!

Request #2: The Riches of His Inheritance

Notice the phrase, "his glorious inheritance in the saints."

When we think of inheritance, we usually think about what we shall receive. But notice, the Apostle Paul is saying that we, the gathered people of God, the saints, are His inheritance. This is consistent with other verses like:

- **Deuteronomy 32:9** - But the Lord's portion is his people, Jacob his allotted heritage.

- **Psalm 33:12** - Blessed is the nation whose God is the Lord, the people whom he has chosen as his heritage!

What I love about this is that Paul is communicating a high value and esteem that God places on us! If we are God's inheritance, then we should live like it! F.F. Bruce says, "Paul prays here that his readers may appreciate the value which God places on them, his plan to accomplish his eternal purpose through them…in order that their lives may be in keeping with this high calling." Knowing God means knowing how He feels about us—that we are His possession and knowing that we are His possession means that we are to live as saints, holy and set apart from the world, yet showing His glory to the world.

When she was young, Queen Victoria was shielded from the fact that she would be the next ruling monarch of England because they didn't want that knowledge to spoil her. When her teacher finally told her that she would one day be the Queen of England, Victoria said, "Then I will be good!"

Knowing we are God's inheritance shouldn't spoil us but spur us on to love and good deeds. It should change how we think about ourselves and our fellow saints as well. It should keep us from thinking too much of ourselves. We can't be prideful because we didn't earn it or deserve it. It should keep us from thinking too little about ourselves. We shouldn't be anxious, because our lives are secured with the fact that we belong to God. We are His inheritance. It should change the way we think of our brothers and sisters in the church, because we together make up the local expression of the body of Christ.

Request #3: The Immeasurable Greatness of His Power

Ephesians 1:19-20 states:

> …and what is the immeasurable greatness of his power toward us who believe, according to the working of his great might that he worked in Christ when he raised him from the dead and seated him at his right hand in the heavenly places…

Paul's prayer is that the church would have a first-hand knowledge of the power of God. In Ephesus, the notion that gods were in total control of one's health, peace, and prosperity permeated the culture. Klyne Snodgrass, in the NIV Commentary on Ephesians notes:

> "This text doesn't give a full explanation of the power and its effect in the lives of believers. Rather, the focus is on freedom from spiritual powers. In the ancient world, people had an extraordinary fear of hostile spiritual powers. Health, love, and success were all at the mercy of spiritual influences."

Paul wanted this church, whom he loved, to be free from the anxious life. When we live anxious lives, we give power to so many things that we think will determine the outcome of our day, of our jobs, of our future and our destiny. Paul says, "No. Don't live that way. Know the Power of God. Live courageously in spite of the dangers and fears you feel."

What are we to know about the power of God? First, the power is called immeasurably great. In other words, we can't fully measure it or explain it. As a child, I experienced this immeasurably great power. I was lying ill in the ICU of a local hospital. I had pneumonia and kidney problems. I was not responding to any of the antibiotics. To make a long story short, my father asked the elders of my church to come and pray over me. They came that evening and prayed for me. Within 45 minutes, I was sitting up and asking for an ice cream sandwich. That moment was the turning point. I didn't feel a surge of energy, or see a light pierce the room in a special way. I just got better. To this day, I can attest that I know that power of God.

Second, the power of God that Paul wants the church to know is compared to the power used to make Jesus our Savior and Lord. Notice the words, "According to," which means, in proportion to, or in a manner corresponding to.

God's power is according to the power used to make Jesus the Savior.

Ephesians 1:20a says:

> …that he worked in Christ when he raised him from the dead…

Jesus is Savior because He conquered sin and death by the resurrection from the dead.

It is also a power according to the power used to make Jesus the Sovereign King or Lord.

Ephesians 1:20b-23 says:

> …and seated him at his right hand in the heavenly places, far above all rule and authority and power and dominion, and above

every name that is named, not only in this age but also in the one to come. And he put all things under his feet and gave him as head over all things to the church, which is his body, the fullness of him who fills all in all.

The power of God that Paul wants the church to know is in accordance with the same power that made Jesus Savior and Sovereign.

To whom is this power directed? The immeasurably great power that Paul wants us to know is directed toward us -- the church, His body. We are called to partner with Him to influence every sphere. We are given the task to influence all arenas with the aroma of Jesus Christ.

When we allow circumstances and agitators to dominate our thinking, we go on the defensive versus playing offense. Like the agitators in Ezra's story, these things cause fear and angst, which keep us from walking in faith. Instead of being bound up, we should turn our faces to the presence of God so that we might know Him more intimately, personally, and powerfully. We must worship. We must know His promises. We must be fueled for the mission He has for us.

One of my favorite Psalms is Psalm 34. It's a call to worship, to trust, and to bask in the presence of God. Let me just share the first ten verses with you. Psalm 34:1-10 states:

> I will bless the Lord at all times;
>   his praise shall continually be in my mouth.
> My soul makes its boast in the Lord;
>   let the humble hear and be glad.
> Oh, magnify the Lord with me,
>   and let us exalt his name together!
> I sought the Lord, and he answered me
>   and delivered me from all my fears.
> Those who look to him are radiant,
>   and their faces shall never be ashamed.
> This poor man cried, and the Lord heard him

and saved him out of all his troubles.
  The angel of the Lord encamps
    around those who fear him, and delivers them.
  Oh, taste and see that the Lord is good!
    Blessed is the man who takes refuge in him!
  Oh, fear the Lord, you his saints,
    for those who fear him have no lack!
  The young lions suffer want and hunger;
    but those who seek the Lord lack no good thing.

As we worship, personally and corporately, God gives us a radiant face. As we boast in the Lord, others hear and are glad. As we seek Him, He delivers us from our fears. His angels encamp around us. His provision is never-ending, and He provides good things.

More than that, we get a vision for more of His rule and reign on earth as it is in heaven. I appreciate the words of Alan Platt, in City Changers, "Fundamentally, the church does not exist for the church itself but rather to affect the world. We don't want to simply attract a crowd—we must move people in their spiritual journey to become lovers of God and agents of change in communities."[24]

That's our goal at CityRise. We are a network of churches and ministries who are seeking to lift our city and the world by generously giving the gospel of Jesus Christ. We do this through mutual collaboration, as the church and para-church lock arms to work together to advance the cause of the gospel and influence our city for good. At our newest campus, CityRise Missouri City, we have built an entire wing of the fellowship building as a clinic for our health care partner, Casa El Buen Samaritano. We are collaborating together to generously provide health care to the poor of our city free of charge. We also are partnering with Attack Poverty to distribute food to those with food insecurity. We are working together with Attack Poverty's afterschool program at the elementary school just up the street to help tutor children and assist their educational needs. We are meeting physical needs and practical needs for an opportunity to meet spiritual needs. These are just small examples of the various ways we are seeking to lift our city.

When we know God intimately, we are moved to the poor, the least, the hurting, and the broken. When we love and serve them generously, God gets glory. May God give us a radiant face as we seek Him that we might in turn serve others for the glory of God! Remember, worship fuels our fight!

REFLECTION QUESTIONS:

1. What do you remember about that first worship service when you returned to corporate worship after the COVID-19 pandemic? What did you experience?

2. What value do you place on corporate worship – low, medium, or high? Why did you answer the way you did?

3. In what ways have you lacked God's peace and power?

4. What steps of personal and corporate worship will you take to bask in the "white-hot glory of God?"

5. What ministry or mission field has God called you to? Are you being faithful to use your influence to show others God's glory and point them to Christ?

CHAPTER 8

Fighting for Faithfulness: A Time to Build Up

Some fights stories are quick. Some last for years. Notice the time element for Jennifer and the faithfulness of God in this fight story.

It was a Sunday morning in February. I don't remember what year. I was on staff at the church, so Sunday mornings were workdays. More often than not, I was seated in the sound booth, available to assist the worship team or preaching pastor with whatever issue that arose. God was gracious in that in the midst of work, I was also able to find moments to engage in worship. Some seasons were easier than others. It had been a long season of infertility for my husband and me. At that point, we were looking at about eight to nine years of doctors, medicines, treatments, miscarriages and just seasons of waiting. It makes you weary. There is an emptiness that you are unable to really explain to others who haven't walked this journey. You simultaneously live in the real world and the "what if" world, in joy for friends and family and grief for yourself.

There is no real sense of when the road will come to an end, either by choice or by achieving the end result: a child.

It had been a trying season. As a female, the journey of infertility plays tricks with your mind. "Maybe I wouldn't be a very good mother, so God is protecting me from myself." "Maybe something bad is going to happen to me, so God is protecting my husband from having to raise a child on his own. Do I even want to be a mother, or is that just what I think I'm supposed to want because society tells me so?" And the ultimate "Maybe there is something wrong with me and I'm just not good enough." Some days I was able to fight through those feelings and doubts, other days they would overtake me. I would give in to the insecurities and the doubts. We had often talked about adoption. In fact, growing up I always said I wanted to adopt. It was this beautiful earthly picture of our Heavenly Father's love for us. But when you are faced with the reality that is your only option you must grieve the loss of any future of an offspring that is a little you and a little your spouse. It can suddenly become an insurmountable hill. And let's be real, they don't make it easy, nor should they. It's a precious life that needs to be protected, but the process is incredibly vulnerable and invasive. It's hard to get excited about it when you are worn down and weary.

I remember sitting on the front row that Sunday morning, in a moment of worship, and hearing within my spirit, not an audible voice but these words, "I'm not asking you to be excited, I'm asking you to be obedient." Gut punch. I'll never forget. And it was this moment that turned the corner for my husband and me. I won't say it was easy. There were days in the next couple years that we doubted and wanted to veer off course. BUT GOD... He was so faithful. And anytime we began to waver, He quietly provided and straightened our path. The story from beginning to end was approximately 12 years. But His timing was perfect – through treatments, the call to pursue adoption, His miraculous financial provision, to the less than 24 hour call to come pick up our daughter and bring her home. It has been nothing more than an overwhelming show of His glory and power to change our story and fight for us.

A friend once told me, "We often overestimate what we can accomplish in a year and underestimate what we can accomplish in ten years." This man is very wise and has led companies at a very high level. Most of our fights aren't ten or twelve-year battles, like Jennifer's, but some are. As I have watched people fight, and fought some myself, I have noted that it always lasts longer and requires more of those in the fight than estimated. As we examine what it takes to stay in the fight, let's consider the element of time.

One of the things that drew me to the Ezra and Nehemiah story is that it's a rebuilding story. The temple was razed and so were the walls of Jerusalem. Many businesses, churches, and organizations find themselves rebuilding. As we opened back up from being shut down from the Coronavirus Pandemic, I told our staff, "You can tear anything down in a day – a career, a marriage, or a high-rise. But it takes seasons to build. It will take us two years to rebuild."

Ecclesiastes 3 speaks of the various seasons that we go through and many of these can be described as battles, struggles, burdens and fights. Ecclesiastes 3:1-8 says:

> For everything there is a season, and a time for every matter under heaven:
> a time to be born, and a time to die;
> a time to plant, and a time to pluck up what is planted;
> a time to kill, and a time to heal;
> a time to break down, and a time to build up;
> a time to weep, and a time to laugh;
> a time to mourn, and a time to dance;
> a time to cast away stones, and a time to gather stones together;
> a time to embrace, and a time to refrain from embracing;
> a time to seek, and a time to lose;
> a time to keep, and a time to cast away;
> a time to tear, and a time to sew;

a time to keep silence, and a time to speak;
a time to love, and a time to hate;
a time for war, and a time for peace.

Nearly every line in this poem describes some sort of struggle, battle or fight. For some women, getting pregnant has been the fight of their lives. Their struggle with infertility has been long, expensive, and an emotional roller coaster. Other people have watched the love of their lives slowly slip out of their hands as cancer or some other ailment has taken its toll. They have fought and advocated and stood guard, only to lose their loved one too soon. Some have planted their lives into their small business battling through a nation-wide shut down striving to stay relevant as everyone pivots. Some have experienced the death of a marriage as their spouse walks out on them leaving them to pick up the pieces.

I wonder if Zerubbabel or Nehemiah, the principal builders in this story, studied Solomon's wisdom. I wonder if either of them got stuck on these words in verse 3 that says, "...and a time to build up."

If you look at the story, the time it took to rebuild the walls and repair the gates of Jerusalem was a drop in the bucket compared to the time it took to rebuild the temple. The walls and gates took 52 days to complete while the temple was constructed over the reign of three different Medo-Persian kings, taking 20 years to complete.

As we compare the narratives, we see similar conditions emerge and different responses. Let's see what we can learn about the time it takes to build up from each section of the story.

ZERUBBABEL'S TEMPLE

In 535 B.C., the Jews began to rebuild the temple. They rebuilt the altar and see that the foundation had not been laid. An offering was taken and the Sidonians and Tyrians are employed to provide supplies just as Solomon had done. Ezra 3:8-13 captures the first milestone of this battle.

Now in the second year after their coming to the house of God at Jerusalem, in the second month, Zerubbabel the son of Shealtiel and Jeshua the son of Jozadak made a beginning, together with the rest of their kinsmen, the priests and the Levites and all who had come to Jerusalem from the captivity. They appointed the Levites, from twenty years old and upward, to supervise the work of the house of the Lord. And Jeshua with his sons and his brothers, and Kadmiel and his sons, the sons of Judah, together supervised the workmen in the house of God, along with the sons of Henadad and the Levites, their sons and brothers.

And when the builders laid the foundation of the temple of the Lord, the priests in their vestments came forward with trumpets, and the Levites, the sons of Asaph, with cymbals, to praise the Lord, according to the directions of David king of Israel. And they sang responsively, praising and giving thanks to the Lord,

"For he is good, for his steadfast love endures forever toward Israel."

And all the people shouted with a great shout when they praised the Lord, because the foundation of the house of the Lord was laid. But many of the priests and Levites and heads of fathers' houses, old men who had seen the first house, wept with a loud voice when they saw the foundation of this house being laid, though many shouted aloud for joy, so that the people could not distinguish the sound of the joyful shout from the sound of the people's weeping, for the people shouted with a great shout, and the sound was heard far away.

What a milestone this must have been. This is that moment when the leaders looked at each other and say, "We've got momentum on our side. Let's push the accelerator to the floor." The young people see the first of what they believe will be many victories. They are elated. They shout for joy. At the same time, the older generation saw that this temple foundation was much smaller than the original temple. They had seen Solomon's Temple in its grandeur and in its prime. This created grief for some of them. But the sentiment of most of the attendants of this dedicatory ceremony was one of elation, as this project was under way, and it would only be a matter of time.

Temptation

As I mentioned in the last chapter the Lord's enemies often come tempting us to compromise. If they can't get us to join them, then they use opposition and oppression to keep us from moving forward. This is where the fight takes on a whole new layer of challenges.

As you fight for the burden to see your child off drugs, as you fight to transform an inner-city community, or as you fight for your marriage, your fight may have to first be with yourself. How easy would it be to say, "Oh, it's just marijuana, it's no big deal?" Or maybe you say of your husband, "He's just being flirtatious with the neighbor. That allows me to flirt with whomever I want as well." As you fight to build your home, your city and the church, be on the lookout for the temptation to compromise. That's what we see in Ezra 4 as the Samaritans approach Zerubbabel and the other leaders and offer a partnership. Ezra 4:1-3 says:

> Now when the adversaries of Judah and Benjamin heard that the returned exiles were building a temple to the Lord, the God of Israel, they approached Zerubbabel and the heads of fathers' houses and said to them, "Let us build with you, for we worship your God as you do, and we have been sacrificing to him ever since the days of Esarhaddon king of Assyria who brought us here." But Zerubbabel, Jeshua, and the rest of the heads of fathers' houses in Israel said to them, "You have nothing to do with us in building a house to our God; but we alone will build to the Lord, the God of Israel, as King Cyrus the king of Persia has commanded us."

You have probably heard that old saying, "If you don't stand for something, you will fall for anything." Fortunately, Zerubbabel and his leadership had a discerning spirit. They sensed that these people were adversaries, who were trying to get the Jews to compromise. Brenamen says:

> As 2 Kings 17:33 points out, this mixed population (including some Jews) "worshiped the LORD, but they also served their own gods in accordance with the customs of the nations from which they had been brought." The exilic or postexilic author of Kings also says: "To this day they persist in their former practices. They neither worship the LORD nor adhere to the decrees and ordinances." In God's sight such "syncretism" is not real worship but is sin and rebellion and would have proved fatal to the spiritual life of the new community. [25]

What happens when we compromise on our ethics or beliefs? That's what the people of Judah were being asked to do. It's also what the church has been tempted to do for centuries. It is no different in our day today. When we compromise on our convictions, we make concessions and shift course. Ultimately, this will delay us from reaching that for which we are fighting.

Compromising our convictions may not feel like and entire change of course, but when we compromise our beliefs, we blend in and diminish what we stand for. Zerubbabel, Joshua, and the other elders were wise enough to know that to compromise and build with these others would have been a great waste of time and energy. It would not have the blessing of God. It would have had the blessing of man, but the Jews motivation was the glory of God, not approval from their neighbors.

Opposition and Cancel Culture

When those who fight against us can't tempt us into compromise, they shift tactics and outwardly oppose us. This is what they did to Zerubbabel and the elders as they had mobilized the rebuilding of the temple. Those who opposed them created fear, discouragement and frustration. Ezra 4:4 says:

> Then the people of the land discouraged the people of Judah and made them afraid to build and bribed counselors against them to frustrate their purpose, all the days of Cyrus king of Persia, even until the reign of Darius king of Persia.

The word afraid here carries with it the idea that the fearful tactics would deter action. The word discouragement comes from two words that when put together convey the idea of lowering the power of one's hands. The word frustrate here means to stop or thwart.

This is what cancel culture looks like – pressure tactics to cause one to stop, to be afraid to move forward, and to slow progress and lower influence. What has God called you to build? If you are experiencing a toxic culture that is seeking to slow you down, create fear in your life, and thwart your purpose, you most likely are building something worthy of the fight you are experiencing.

Their threats are, "I'll tie this up in court for years," and, "I'll ruin you." Their tactics worked, as lawyers were hired, and this declaration went to court. Wiersbe says, "The people of the land hired men at court to resist the Jews, and this device succeeded in stopping the work...For nearly fifteen years (534-520) the work ceased on the temple." [26]

Those who oppose the Jews kept this tied up until the second year of the reign of King Darius (522-486). After this lengthy delay, the Lord stirred in their hearts once again.

EMBOLDENED BY THE WORD OF THE LORD

I remember the day when the Lord spoke to me. It was July 2019. I was on a two-week study break given to me by the church to set aside time to pray, plan, and seek the heart of God. I had spent some time in the Scriptures that morning and written in my journal.

I was laying out sermon series for the coming months and decided to go on a jog.

I was on a jogging path around 10:30 in the morning. It was hot and humid. I was all alone. As I was jogging, I heard a voice say, "We're not comfortable with sacrifice." I knew it was the Lord, but I stopped and looked around to make sure it wasn't someone passing me at my slow pace. I immediately grabbed my phone and opened my notes app. Thoughts began to flood my mind. The Emmanuel Baptist Church of Missouri City was the very first thought that came to me. I began to log any and everything that I could think of about that. But I knew it was time to take our relationship with Pastor Justo and his sweet congregation to the next level.

What had kept us from moving further faster? What had kept us from just making this happen? It was now almost five years after we had begun to converse. Why had we taken so long to move ahead?

I still ask myself those questions. I have some rational answers. First, as we began to roll this out in 2015, we had a significant economic downturn in the oil and gas markets. We believed it wouldn't be financially prudent to stick ourselves out there. Fortunately, we had some resources we could invest each year for the next few years, and we bought ourselves some time. But was that a lack of faith or God's providence?

Then, we hit a few seasons of crises at our inner loop campuses– land swap discussions with one of the city governments that didn't go well; a significant staff crisis; Hurricane Harvey flooding nearly 100 families' homes of our congregants. Then, at the Missouri City campus, there was a pipe that burst in the back building and the insurance company tried to take advantage of Pastor Justo and his congregation with a low-ball, quick payout. Fortunately, we had a team who could advocate for their church. But this tied the transition up for over two years.

But now, in 2019, we were just humming along. The resources from the insurance company were in. We were well recovered from the natural disaster. Things were so delayed, I just wasn't sure what we were supposed to do.

FROM CLOUDINESS TO CLARITY

I learned somewhere along the way that when you can't see the entire picture, keep walking, as the cloudiness will ultimately part and clarity will come. Fortunately, we had continued to walk with Pastor Justo. When the Lord spoke to me, I knew we needed to act and be faithful to that word.

Notice the word of the Lord from Haggai the prophet. Haggai 1:7-9 states:

> "Thus says the Lord of hosts: Consider your ways. Go up to the hills and bring wood and build the house, that I may take pleasure in it and that I may be glorified, says the Lord. You looked for much, and behold, it came to little. And when you brought it home, I blew it away. Why? declares the Lord of hosts. Because of my house that lies in ruins, while each of you busies himself with his own house."

These words are convicting, aren't they? It is easy to busy ourselves to build our own homes and neglect the word of the Lord that declares that He wants glory in His house. I think of the parable of the great banquet where the master invites all the guests, but they were too busy. So, the master tells his servants to go to others. They too were too busy. Then the master commands his servants to go to the highways and byways to gather anyone who will come, "that my house may be filled," (Luke 14:23).

God still wants his house filled. He wants His servants to go wherever we must to invite others in. When the Lord came to me saying, "We aren't comfortable with sacrifice," I knew the cloudiness had just lifted. It was time to take the next steps.

Notice the next steps of Zerubbabel and Joshua. Haggai 1:12-15 says:

> Then Zerubbabel the son of Shealtiel, and Joshua the son of Jehozadak, the high priest, with all the remnant of the people, obeyed the voice of the Lord their God, and the words of Haggai the prophet, as the Lord their God had sent him. And the people feared the Lord. Then Haggai, the messenger of the Lord, spoke to the people with the Lord's message, "I am with you, declares the Lord." And the Lord stirred up the spirit of Zerubbabel the son of Shealtiel, governor of Judah, and the spirit of Joshua the son of Jehozadak, the high priest, and the spirit of all the remnant of the people. And they came and worked on the house of the Lord of hosts, their God, on the twenty-fourth day of the month, in the sixth month, in the second year of Darius the king.

Before we move on from this part of the story, don't miss what you may need to hear right now as you fight. When we are compelled by God's word, we should act and obey. Go to your Sherebiah's that are walking with you and say, "Here is what I believe God has just spoken to me. I know I set this down for a time, but He is stirring me to pick it up again." Ask them to give you counsel. Seek affirmation from their walk with God. Second, believe that God is with you.

I recall being stuck in a season of doubt. There was pain associated with it and a sense that I had gone as far as I could. We were out of the crisis, but it wasn't without my own battle wounds. My friend, Brian Haynes, pastor of Bay Area Church in Houston was, along with his wife Angela, doing a marriage event for us. Brian took us through a wonderful teaching and then asked us to answer some questions and listen for the voice of the Lord.

I reluctantly did the exercise as I really didn't want to answer the questions he was posing. Frankly, I didn't want to know the answers to the questions. But I did it anyway. This pain I was processing didn't have anything to do with my marriage. It was pain associated with my leadership journey. So, I wrote out the answers to his questions and then did what he asked – I listened for the voice of the Lord. Do you know what I heard? "But Roger, I am with you."

Thirteen times in the Old Testament alone, we see these words, "I am with you, declares the Lord." Maybe today, in the midst of this fight you didn't pick, but that showed up at your front doorstep, you need to simply be reminded that the Lord, the God of Heaven, the Great I Am, the One who is the same yesterday, today and forever, is with you. So, stay in the fight!

20 YEARS VS. 52 DAYS

From start to finish, when Nehemiah is wrecked with his burden, to when the walls and gates are rebuilt, we see the passage of almost nine months. His burden lasts four months. His journey to Jerusalem lasts three months. After three days in the city of Jerusalem, he mobilizes the people to rebuild the walls from start to finish in a period of 52 days. It's an incredible story.

The fight story to build the temple was a marathon. The fight to build the walls and gates of Jerusalem was a sprint. It began when Nehemiah arrived in Jerusalem with an escort of soldiers and supplies. Clearly, he was up to something because, as Nehemiah 2:10 notes, "But when Sanballat the Horonite and Tobiah the Ammonite servant heard this, it displeased them greatly that someone had come to seek the welfare of the people of Israel."

Coming into the region on horseback with an army escort was one thing. Nehemiah acquired the necessary timber from Asaph, the keeper of the king's forest, to rebuild the ten gates of the city. After being in Jerusalem for three days, he went out with a few men at night and surveyed the walls and gates of the city. Nehemiah 2:16 says:

> And the officials did not know where I had gone or what I was doing, and I had not yet told the Jews, the priests, the nobles, the officials, and the rest who were to do the work.

The Importance of Timing

Isn't it interesting that Nehemiah only shared his burden with King Artaxerxes? The king's letters may have revealed his plan to the governors and those who handled the supplies. Maybe the officers who had taken the journey with him knew what he was about to do. I love how Nehemiah just sat quietly even as he arrived into town. Clearly, he was there for a reason. It appeared that he is letting anticipation build, so that at just the right time, he could cast the vision of rebuilding the walls and the gates.

Leadership expert, John C. Maxwell says this about timing, "The right thing at the wrong time is the wrong thing every time." This is a creative way of expressing how significant and important it is to get your timing down. Had Nehemiah come in from the first moment he arrived, he would have encountered tremendous resistance. He knew he couldn't restore the walls himself. He knew he needed the people to take ownership of the task.

At just the right time, after creating tension in the lives of the nobles and officials, the priests and the other Jews who would be doing the work, Nehemiah says in Nehemiah 2:17:

> Then I said to them, "You see the trouble we are in, how Jerusalem lies in ruins with its gates burned. Come, let us build the wall of Jerusalem, that we may no longer suffer derision."

As Nehemiah casts the vision, he begins with the problem. It's the obvious problem. No one had the capacity to fix prior to this. It's the kind of problem that if you don't have the governor and king's approval, you will get yourself killed. It's the kind of problem that keeps you oppressed by your adversaries because you have no way to truly defend yourself. He says, "Guys, here's the trouble we are in – the walls are in ruin and the gates are burned up."

Nehemiah then invites them to join in to solve the problem together. He says, "Come, let us build...that we may no longer suffer…" Notice also, that he says in verse 18, "And I told them of the hand of my God that had been upon me for good, and also of the words that the king had spoken to me."

The way Nehemiah handles this burden intrigues me. From start to finish, he handles it with great reverence. He fasts and prays and then goes before the king. As he comes to Jerusalem and surveys the land and talks to the people, there is a sense that he knows that he is just a steward of the moment and situation. He's not intimidated. He's not overwhelmed by the task at hand. He's simply doing his job and inviting others to join him. As a steward, he is going to leave it better than he found it.

Isn't that the invitation of Jesus to us as well? How can you influence in such a way as to leave this part of God's kingdom, this part of the city, or this part of the church better than you found it? The commendation of Jesus that so many believers want to hear is, "Well done, good and faithful servant."

I hope it is obvious how madly in love I am with my wife, Julee. I am captivated by her. She's gorgeous, both inside and out and I love doing life with her. She is very smart. She is the budget director of one of our local school districts and since COVID-19, she and her team have been working non-stop to support the 50,000 students and employees of the district. One of Julee's gifts is seeing the big picture and the depth of the problem at hand. As Mike Bonem and I say in Leading from the Second Chair, Julee has mastered the Deep-Wide Paradox. She knows how to navigate the broad challenges and helps others see how all the pieces fit together. But more than anything, I have noted that wherever she goes, things get better. She would hate for me to write this for so many to read, but it's a great example of what faithfulness looks like. Faithful stewardship lifts. Faithful stewardship fights to improve things. Faithful stewardship seeks to multiply impact. At least that's what the two and five talent stewards did in the parable of the talents. They brought their talent to need and opportunity and there was improvement, impact, and increase.

FAITHFULNESS IS OUR GOAL IN THE FIGHT

Countless times I have looked in the eyes of a friend or church member during their fights and said to them, "You want to be able to look in the mirror and say, 'I did everything that I could to win

this fight.'" Our sweet friends Rick and Sheri went through a very difficult battle with cancer that ultimately took Sheri from us. When they discovered her cancer, it had already spread to the liver, and this was causing so many problems.

Early in the journey, as Rick and I would talk, Rick would share about the course of treatment and how it was going. I could sense frustration with a lack of coordination, yet Rick didn't seem to want to rock the boat. I said to him, "Rick, she can't advocate for herself. You have got to. Don't worry about offending the doctors. Fight for her. If their offense is more important than your wife, they aren't acting in her best interest anyway." Rick received my counsel which freed him up to advocate more aggressively. Ultimately, I said to him, "Rick, this may not turn out like we want it to, but you want to be able to know that you did all that you could possibly do to fight for Sheri."

I can say that Rick was faithful to the end. I was so proud of him and the way that he fought for his sweet bride, for his whole family, and for God to be glorified. He was faithful to the end.

Faithfulness Stirs Others to Join In

Nehemiah's faithfulness stirred the hearts of those who had been living under these dangerous living conditions. In many ways, his invitation to them was to join in on what they already knew that they wanted and needed. He now had the resources at hand. He just needed their buy-in.

Look at their response in Nehemiah 2:18b:

And they said, "Let us rise up and build." So they strengthened their hands for the good work.

Some people just need permission to join in. I was at the airport in Birmingham, Alabama and I remember standing in a long line to check luggage. As with many airlines, this airline had scaled back the staff needed to receive bags and tried to automate the process through kiosk service stations. The problem with this line is that people assumed the kiosks, which were at the counter, were only for the person at the front of the line. Other airlines see how this has created a back log in lines and have moved their kiosks out to where the people are before they ever get to the counter.

As we stood in line for a handful of minutes, it became clear that the people checking in at the front of the line were having difficulty. The attendant had learned the art of ignoring the rest of the line. We were left there to wait and wait even though there were multiple kiosks open at the counter. Everything communicated, though open, stay put until it's your turn.

After a few more minutes, one of the people in line walked up to the front of the line and graciously asked, "Are these other kiosks open?" To which the attendant replied, "Absolutely. Please use them." We did, and this moved the line along and got people through security and to their gates on time.

Most people need permission to move. Others see a problem and begin to tackle it, then ask for permission. The people living in Jerusalem simply needed the permission to create the change they knew that they needed. They needed permission to fight and once they had it, they fought with great fervor.

Faithfulness isn't Surprised by Opposition

Almost immediately in this narrative, the antagonists are revealed as Sanballat the Horonite and Tobiah the Ammonite. These are men of influence and power. Brenamen tell us:

"Sanballat the Horonite" probably was from one of the Beth-horons about eighteen miles northwest of Jerusalem, although some suggest the Moabite town of Horonaim. According to an Elephantine Papyrus, Sanballat was governor of Samaria in 408 B.C. Since his sons were acting for him at that time, he probably was elderly. These verses imply that he already was governor of Samaria in Nehemiah's time.

"Tobiah the Ammonite official" was likely governor of Ammon, although he may have been an Ammonite official under Sanballat's authority. Tobiah is a Jewish name and not Ammonite, but the Tobiad family was to have influence in Ammon for a long time. These Tobiads may have been descendants of the Tobiah who in

Ezra 2:60 was rejected from the Jewish community because "they could not show that their families were descended from Israel." If so, their long-standing enmity against the Jewish community may have begun at that time.

Earlier in the reign of Artaxerxes their complaints against Jerusalem had been accepted by the king, who decreed that the Jews stop building. So a Jew coming now as governor, with authorization to build, greatly disturbed them.[27]

Notice their reaction when they discover the Jews are about to rebuild Jerusalem. Nehemiah 2:19 says:

But when Sanballat the Horonite and Tobiah the Ammonite servant and Geshem the Arab heard of it, they jeered at us and despised us and said, "What is this thing that you are doing? Are you rebelling against the king?"

Then in chapter 4:1-2, it says:

Now when Sanballat heard that we were building the wall, he was angry and greatly enraged, and he jeered at the Jews. And he said in the presence of his brothers and of the army of Samaria,

"What are these feeble Jews doing? Will they restore it for themselves? Will they sacrifice? Will they finish up in a day? Will they
revive the stones out of the heaps of rubbish, and burned ones at
that?"

In both chapters, Sanballat and Tobiah, jeered, or mocked Nehemiah and the Jews. They began with mocking and ridicule. They
assaulted them with words to try to get them to stand down. It's not
unlike social media today or what the press does to someone who
doesn't think like they do. Warren Wiersbe says, "Whenever the
people of God start doing the work of God, there will be opposition. A worker of weak faith and purpose will quit, but a person of
resolution and confidence will overcome the opposition and finish
the task." In these chapters, Nehemiah will encounter the opposition
of cancel culture and show us how to persevere in building that to
which we have been called. Here are the ways Nehemiah and the
Jews faced opposition:

- Ridicule (4:1-6)
- Force (4:7-9)
- Discouragement (4:10)
- Fear (4:11-23)
- Selfishness (5)
- Guile (6:1-4)
- Slander (6:5-9)
- Threats (6:10-19)

What's a good response to opposition? What's the right response
to ridicule or slander or threats?

Two proverbs stand side by side when dealing with this sort of
thing. They are Proverbs 26:4-5, which says:

> Answer not a fool according to his folly,
>   lest you be like him yourself.
> Answer a fool according to his folly,
>   lest he be wise in his own eyes.

This isn't the first time I have wrestled with this question. In, *A Minute of Vision for Men: 365 Motivational Moments to Kick-Start Your Day*, I wrote about this question illustrating it with some events from the gridiron. I'll share that with you here:

Which Is It?

Football is such an emotional game that periodically players' tempers explode on the sidelines. These fuming players go off on others and get in their faces. It is interesting to see that at times, those being confronted will just stand there and say nothing, looking past the maniac, onto the field of play. It reminds me of Proverbs 26:4, which says, "Don't answer the foolish arguments of fools, or you will become as foolish as they are."

Then there are other times when the fool must be confronted. This happened during the Cowboys' 2015 season when Greg Hardy, the troubled pass rusher, exploded on the special teams unit and their coach after another blown play that caused the Cowboys to fall behind again.

Another embattled player, known for his own struggles, Dez Bryant, couldn't take it anymore and confronted Hardy. The wild scene became fodder for the network analysts later that day and well into the following week.

You see, after a time or two of a fool's ranting, it is appropriate to stand up to him and put him in his place. That is why I think it is fascinating that the very next verse, Proverbs 26:5, tells us to confront the fool: "Be sure to answer the foolish arguments of fools, or they will become wise in their own estimation."

Which is it? There is a time to let it go and a time to confront. Discerning which it is requires great wisdom. Maybe consider seeking wise counsel from an outside voice before confronting the fool. Their lack of proximity to the situation may be exactly what you need.[28]

How did Nehemiah deal with the opposition? The simple answer is that he didn't let it deter him. He knew what his mission was. He stuck to it. Every time the adversaries came to him, he didn't tuck his tail, nor did he come off the wall. Instead, he fortified himself and the people and continued the great task to restore the city. Nehemiah knew if he could finish the task and restore the city, the oppressors' power would be taken away.

Faithfulness is the Long Game

Let's talk about time and faithfulness. Nehemiah's faithfulness wasn't just a 52-day run. He had been building faithfulness for a long time. The very fact that he could leave his position as cup bearer and become the governor showed tremendous trust. This trust is built a day at a time as you faithfully show up and contribute. As a person of influence, you are either making deposits into your trust account or you are taking deposits out of it.

I had the chance to spend some time with Dr. Ed Young of Second Baptist Church in Houston recently. He was so gracious as we met in his office and talked about leading through current ministry dynamics. I listened and noted many things. One of the things that impressed me the most is that in his 80's, Dr. Young still is young at heart. He is more passionate about reaching people than he has ever been before. They were in the midst of a $38 million campaign for a new children's building. He told me of some other exciting initiatives they had planned. We chatted about what the church was like in the 1970s when he came to Houston to pastor Second Baptist. It was a fascinating time for me as a fellow pastor in the city.

One of my big take-a-ways was the picture of faithfulness over time. I am sure he has had his ups and downs. I am sure there have been many challenges. I'm not saying any of us have to keep working into our 80's to be considered faithful. That's not it. I'm saying, even into his 80's I was struck by a man who had the same heart that he had in his 40's, 50's, and 60's. It challenged me.

After the wall was built, Nehemiah still led as a servant who had been entrusted with his master's riches. Frankly, I think that is the secret to his long-term success as governor in Jerusalem. He knew he wasn't the owner, just the representative. He knew his assignment would one day come to an end. He knew he had the capacity to leave it better. He showed up each day to do just that—to build faithfulness over the long-haul.

REFLECTION QUESTIONS:

1. Go back and read Ecclesiastes 3:1-8. Which of these seasons do you identify with the most and why?

2. What type of temptations to compromise have you experienced in the last year? Did you compromise your convictions, or did you stand fast? What have you learned from this experience?

3. Have you ever experienced opposition while trying to restore something that was broken? If so, what did you experience? From whom? Why do you think they opposed you?

4. Is it better to not answer a fool in his folly or to answer a fool in his folly? How might Nehemiah's response help us see how we should proceed when faced with opposition?

5. Who is an example of faithfulness in your life? What outstanding characteristics do they possess and how might you cultivate those characteristics in your life?

SECTION 4

Fight for Your City: Linking Arms to Lift the City

As we get into this fight story, I want to introduce you to Brandon Baca, the CEO of Attack Poverty. Brandon moved from the second chair to the first inside his own organization after his longtime friend and boss took his own life. In our first conversation after Brandon took the lead, one month after this tragic moment in so many lives, and a few days after the COVID-19 virus began to spread across the globe, I had a chance to listen to Brandon. He believed in the mission of Attack Poverty, but he also felt the weight of his new role. With only two weeks of income in the bank, donors were unsure of how Attack Poverty would move forward. A global crisis called on every organization to pivot. Knowing what to do next was daunting. Pretty quickly, Brandon realized Attack Poverty was more relevant in that moment than it had ever been before.

I had just returned from traveling and working with our teams in Uganda and India. I was on a long flight home and ready to be with my family. It was the beginning of a new year. I knew God was doing great things through our ministry and in my life. I was excited! Then, just a couple weeks later my dear friend and the founder of our organization committed suicide. A few weeks after that COVID-19 was spreading and on the verge of being a global pandemic. I found myself wondering, "What's next?" My world was rocked at the core.

Now, as the newly named CEO of our organization, in the midst of tragedy and crisis, I couldn't help but wonder where God was. I felt alone, afraid, and deeply in pain. I lost my friend! We had to completely rework our programmatic model. Our communities (here and around the world) were hurting and experiencing great needs. I needed to hear from God.

I remember one morning when I walked in my closet to get dressed. I didn't even turn the light on. I just fell to the floor and began to weep. "God, where are you? I need to hear from you, I can't do this without you." In that moment God's still, gentle voice reminded me, "I am with you, I will never leave you." This is what I needed.

God started to provide significant relationships in my life that would lay the foundation for what appeared to be impossible. The fight was on. I was ready. I was scared, but ready. I believed Jesus was there with me and us, leading me and us, and calling me and the Attack Poverty family to step out into the chaotic waters for some of the most challenging years ahead.

In the first nine months of the pandemic, Attack Poverty's staff and volunteers, in cooperation with local charities, churches, and governmental agencies, touched the lives of over 260,000 people in the greater Houston area.

LINKING ARMS, NOT CARING WHO GETS THE CREDIT

In Nehemiah chapter three, the residents of Jerusalem from the priests to the craftsmen link arms and repair the walls and gates of their city. You can visualize the one chronicling the rebuild essentially going section by section until the entire city is accounted for. Here is a sample of this recording of participants in Nehemiah 3:1-4:

> Then Eliashib the high priest rose up with his brothers the priests, and they built the Sheep Gate. They consecrated it and set its doors. They consecrated it as far as the Tower of the Hundred, as far as the Tower of Hananel. And next to him the men of Jericho built. And next to them Zaccur the son of Imri built.
>
> The sons of Hassenaah built the Fish Gate. They laid its beams and set its doors, its bolts, and its bars. And next to them Meremoth the son of Uriah, son of Hakkoz repaired. And next to them Meshullam the son of Berechiah, son of Meshezabel repaired. And next to them Zadok the son of Baana repaired.

What could happen when the people of God joined forces, linked arms together and went all in for the good of their city? What could be if we together sought the welfare of our city?

I believe that our city would be lifted. You see, Proverbs 11 gives us a principle of city-lifting in the first part of verses 10 and 11.

> Proverbs 11:10a (NIV) - When the righteous prosper, the city rejoices…
>
> Proverbs 11:11a (NIV) - Through the blessing of the upright a city is exalted…

Alan Platt, in his book, City Changers says, “Fundamentally, the church does not exist for the church itself, but rather to affect the world. We don’t want to simply attract a crowd—we must move people in their spiritual journeys to become lovers of God and agents of change in communities." [29]

I believe that there is a stewardship to our prosperity that God expects from His people. You see, something happens in cities when righteous people prosper and steward it well. Proverbs 11 above teaches that when the upright experience blessing and decide to pour out blessing, a city is lifted.

Platt argues this when he challenges the church and her leaders to think differently. He says:

> Sometimes in the Bible, God looks at cities and even whole nations as collectives, as single units. In the West, we tend to think of Christianity as an individualistic relationship between one person and one Savior. While that's certainly true, it's not the only way God thinks of humanity.

> Could it be that Jesus meant the church to think not only in terms of personal salvation experiences and personals discipleship but also in terms of salvation and discipleship coming to whole cities? To whole nations?

> Our mentality has to change. We have to stop preaching to people only to encourage them to a better life and the hope that we will all go to heaven one day. We need to empower people to affect communities, to affect their world… our theology must move from a focus only on personal salvation to an understanding of the kingdom engaging all creation." [30]

So, how do we make the shift? How do we live in such a way as to lift our city?

CHAPTER 9

The Fight for Provision: We Must Resource the Fight

My dear friend David feels the weight of stewardship like few people I know. Listen to how he reflects on his journey of learning to fight his battles. He writes:

> What is our purpose in life? I have to remind myself daily that it's not about me. It's about Him. I want to see Christ glorified in all that I do. It's about a calling, a sense of responsibility, recognizing the truth of, "…to whom much is given, much is required." I long to hear the words found in Matthew, "Well done good and faithful servant."
>
> Nowhere does the Bible say life will be a bed of roses. In fact life can be hard at times, confusing, and overwhelming. One of my biggest lessons in life is the need to fight. Everyone who perseveres in the Lord has to recognize we are at WAR. Therefore, we

need to prepare for battle daily. Missing this biblical truth makes life even harder.

Satan wants to devour us. The world will distract us. Our sin will destroy our communion with our Father in Heaven. We must have a plan for battle. We must start from a place of victory. The work of Christ on the cross defeated death and Satan forever. If He is for us who can be against us?

Even knowing all of this, Satan still daily tries to remind me that I'm not enough. The world distracts and overwhelms me leaving me defeated on many days. And that's all before I get to my selfish flesh and desires.

Therefore, I strive to increase my intimacy with the Lord to win the daily battles of life. To do this,

- I walk in a daily relationship with the Father, remembering my identity as a child of God. I spend time lingering with the Father.
- I pray the Serenity Prayer, learning to control the things that I can control and release the rest to God, asking for the wisdom to know the difference.
- I prepare for battle daily by putting on the full armor of God.
- I spend ample time in God's word and learn to use the sword in my life.
- I develop a consistent prayer life, using the Lord's Prayer as a guide.
- I memorize Scripture, fixing my gaze on Christ, and setting my mind on things that are noble and true in order to make no provisions for the flesh.

I live in a state of need and dependency, as God is my supplier and therefore I am a receiver. I'm not a manufacturer, but a receiver and distributer making assisted lay-ups from the Father.

Father fill me so that I can live in overflow bringing glory to your name.

This is how I fight my battles.

When we began our journey together, I shared one of my core convictions – that you are a person of influence and that you will use your influence for good or for bad. In that introduction, I asked you not limit your fight to yourself or your home. I also connected your fight and influence to the church as the place where we are built up. I pushed a bit more, asking you to keep your heart and mind open to the call of Jesus as salt and light, the city on a hill. I know that was many pages ago, but I want us to take a minute to connect the dots if we may.

If our cities are ever going to be lifted, it is because the very people who fill our pews also recognize their stewardship to do something significant together both for the house of God and for the city. Where vision often gets stifled and derailed is around resources. The vision is so big, but we don't see where the resources are for the vision to be realized. We ask the question, how will we pay for all of this? When we don't know, we get stuck. But provision and resources are never a problem for God.

PROVISION IS ON THE WAY

Asking how we will pay for all of this is a natural question. I'm sure it was on the minds of the Jews when the declaration to return to Jerusalem and rebuild the temple was made. But as you read the story, you see that provision was already on the way. Yes, the king levied a tax. That's what kings do. But notice the fact that he also made an offering. It wasn't just any offering, but instead, it was all the articles of the temple that Nebuchadnezzar had taken as his own and put into the house of his gods. This was what kings did. When they invaded and then dominated a people, they would take the articles of their temples and seize them. They would then deposit them in their own temple to declare that their god was greater than the gods of the land that they had just seized. It was a way to both humiliate and dominate a people.

But notice what Cyrus does, as we turn back to the beginning of this story. Ezra 1:4-11 states:

> "And let each survivor, in whatever place he sojourns, be assisted by the men of his place with silver and gold, with goods and with beasts, besides freewill offerings for the house of God that is in Jerusalem."
>
> Then rose up the heads of the fathers' houses of Judah and Benjamin, and the priests and the Levites, everyone whose spirit God had stirred to go up to rebuild the house of the Lord that is in Jerusalem. And all who were about them aided them with vessels of silver, with gold, with goods, with beasts, and with costly wares, besides all that was freely offered. Cyrus the king also brought out the vessels of the house of the Lord that Nebuchadnezzar had carried away from Jerusalem and placed in the house of his gods. Cyrus king of Persia brought these out in the charge of Mithredath the treasurer, who counted them out to Sheshbazzar the prince of Judah. And this was the number of them: 30 basins of gold, 1,000 basins of silver, 29 censers, 30 bowls of gold, 410 bowls of silver, and 1,000 other vessels; all the vessels of gold and of silver were 5,400. All these did Sheshbazzar bring up, when the exiles were brought up from Babylonia to Jerusalem.

What Cyrus did was liberating. In returning the articles of the temple, he was declaring liberty for the Jews. But also notice the words freely and freewill. Verse four says, "And let each survivor, in whatever place he sojourns, be assisted by the men of his place with silver and gold, with goods and with beasts, besides freewill offerings for the house of God that is in Jerusalem."

When the people of God gather their resources for the glory of God, the collective impact is exponential. Cyrus, at a minimum, is

instructing the Jews to join in and give of their resources, of both
goods and beasts, for the glory of God. Was this the tithe that he
knew they would have paid anyway? Was this a tax? I'm not sure it
matters. Cyrus knew that the people needed to be involved in this
great work.

But what is interesting to this text is that we do see a phrase that
says, "…besides the freewill offerings for the house of God…" This
freewill offering was a voluntary gift given over and above required
tithes, according to the Lord's blessing upon a person (Dt. 16:10).
They were given freely at one of three feasts each year – the Feast
of Unleavened Bread, the Feast of Weeks, and the Feast of Booths.
Every year every male was to show up at each of these feasts and
worship the Lord. All of this was about to be reinstituted, by the
time you get to Ezra chapter three, the altar is being rebuilt, the
Feast of Booths is celebrated, and the freewill offerings are sacrificed.
But what we must see and teach is this: we are not to come to the
worship of God empty-handed. Instead, we are to give according to
our ability. Deuteronomy 16:16-17 states:

> Three times a year all your males shall appear before the Lord
> your God at the place that he will choose: at the Feast of Unleav-
> ened Bread, at the Feast of Weeks, and at the Feast of Booths.
> They shall not appear before the Lord empty-handed. Every man
> shall give as he is able, according to the blessing of the Lord your
> God that he has given you.

God prescribed this sacrificial system to Israel so as a nation, she
would know that everything she possessed came from the hand of
God – her redemption, her freedom, her land, and her ability to
produce wealth. As you track this story, from the opening para-
graphs of Ezra, through the end of Nehemiah, you see provision.
Here, Cyrus challenged the Jews to freely join their brothers and sisters and make provision for them as they return to Jerusalem. Quite
often it's through the corporate gathering of the people of God that
provision comes.

GENEROUS, COMMITTED PEOPLE CAN ACCOMPLISH THE UNTHINKABLE

When Nehemiah was gripped with the vision to go to Jerusalem and rebuild her walls, I doubt he thought that this project could be completed in 52 days. But he had a willing people who navigated adversity, followed his lead, and were steadfast to the end. He led them well. They availed themselves to the work. He proclaimed the vision, showed them what had been provided, and invited them to participate as well. They availed themselves and accomplished something that hadn't been done for a couple of generations.

Have you made yourself available to God lately? It's interesting to note that not everyone will give themselves to what God is doing. When the wall was being rebuilt, it says in Nehemiah 3:5:

> And next to them the Tekoites repaired, but their nobles would not stoop to serve their Lord.

How often is God simply looking for our availability? How many times this past week did God want to do something through you to lift another—a coworker, a family member, a fellow church member, or someone at the grocery store? Are you willing to stoop low to serve the Lord? Are you willing to allow his generosity to flow through you to others? This is a key question when it comes to our own fight stories.

THE CASCADE OF GENEROUS LEADERSHIP

I want to share with you some principles about generosity that I believe are transformative. But before I do, I am convinced that there is a proper order to our being generous. Gordon McDonald helps us with the definition of generosity. He says, "Generosity is sacrificing something of value to us for the good of another, because we love them."[31] This is what differentiates generosity and giving. Giving can be done begrudgingly and devoid of life. But true generosity is always initiated by love.

The cascade of generous leadership starts with my own walk with Jesus. I receive freely and then I am to give freely. I give my tithe to the Lord, knowing this confesses His gospel, as Jesus, the clean One was sacrificed for me, the unclean one.

Then, I come to this realization that if I am going to be generous with others as the Lord is generous with me, then my generosity must begin at home. It's me and Jesus. This overflows out to me and Julee. I love to lead with yes as often as I can. I love to give to my wife. I'm not stingy toward her while lavishing on others. To be a person of integrity, I seek to lead with yes at home with her and then when I can with our kids.

This cascade of leading then flows out to the church staff, the church leadership, the congregation and out to the community and beyond, as generosity ought to be a natural overflow of our walk with Jesus Christ. Generous leaders seek to serve, give, and lower themselves, all in an attempt to lift others. Before we move on, do those closest to you describe you as generous?

All throughout this story, we see resources that were made readily available. In Ezra 1, Cyrus makes an offering and entreats others to do the same. He returns the furnishings of the temple that Nebuchadnezzar had taken when he led the Jews away in captivity.

When Nehemiah makes his request to the king, the timber is given to restore the ten gates of the city. Further, Nehemiah refuses to take the daily food allotment of the governor that he was entitled to so that he wouldn't put any extra expense upon the people. When we look to the words of Jesus, we see that he said so much about money and how it competes for our heart. When the Apostle Paul instructs us on money, he extends an invitation into the life that is truly life. That's what I want for me and that's what I want for you. I want us to experience the life that is truly life.

Notice how 1 Timothy 6:17-19 describes generosity as the life that is truly life.

> As for the rich in this present age, charge them not to be haughty, nor to set their hopes on the uncertainty of riches, but on God, who richly provides us with everything to enjoy. They are to do good, to be rich in good works, to be generous and ready to share, thus storing up treasure for themselves as a good foundation for the future, so that they may take hold of that which is truly life.

Notice the last statement of verse 19 where it describes the life of generosity as one where you can, "… take hold of that which is truly life."

Chip Ingram, in his book, The Genius of Generosity, takes us back to the Hebrew and Greek of the term generosity to help us understand this. In Hebrew, to be generous is to saturate with water, a symbol of life. It carries with it the idea of overflowing in a way that brings life to people. In Greek, generosity means one who is ready to distribute, being available to give time, talent, and treasures to bless others. Ingram says, "When you put all of these together you start to get a dramatic picture of a life that is overflowing with care and concern for others." When we begin to live this way, we realize four key things that compel us forward in our walk with God.

Generosity Changes Our Lives[32]

When we avail ourselves and our resources something significant happens. First, we will find that generosity will change our lives. In Acts 20:35, the Apostle Paul quotes the words of Jesus when he said:

> "In all things I have shown you that by working hard in this way we must help the weak and remember the words of the Lord Jesus, how he himself said, 'It is more blessed to give than to receive.'"

It is more blessed, or "better" to give. Now, if Jesus says something is better, I want it. In Proverbs 11, we see the promise of a generous man prospering. Proverbs 11:25 proclaims:

> Whoever brings blessing will be enriched,
> and one who waters will himself be watered.

The New International Version translates it this way:

> A generous man will prosper;
> he who refreshes others will himself be refreshed.

This proverb tells us that those who are generous prosper. This word literally means to be FAT! The idea is that the generous person overflows with an abundance. I want to have an abundance and I also want to be refreshed. That is available to us through giving of ourselves.

While generosity changes our lives, the inverse is also true. A lack of generosity changes our lives. Have you ever heard of Ebenezer Scrooge? Ebenezer Scrooge shows us that a greedy and stingy heart ends up empty, but the Scripture declares that the generous heart ends up full.

Generosity Connects Us with Others

Our staff evangelist and one of our Spanish campus pastors is named Rick Vasquez. When we met, Pastor Rick was the Pastor of Vision City Church, a bilingual church plant renting space from one of our sister churches nearby. Pastor Rick reached out to me via e-mail and asked if he could have some time with me.

Through our conversations we have developed a friendship and a mentoring relationship where I am able to pour into him, challenge him, and encourage him. But here is the deal: I receive much more than I give. You see, Pastor Rick spent nearly 20 years of his life in the penitentiary. We come from totally different places. Because I was generous with my time, we are now connected to a type of ministry that we didn't have before Pastor Rick came along. Nearly every time I am with him, I hear of people being saved, someone being rescued, and progress for the kingdom. Now, we get to be involved in all sorts of ministry that we never would have been a part of if we hadn't gotten together.

One Christmas, Pastor Rick did an outreach via Angel Tree, a ministry to families of someone who is incarcerated. A friend of mine who is very generous and loves to give away turkeys for Christmas got involved. On his own one year, he gave over 2,000 turkeys away.

Another friend who wanted to provide children Christmas presents got involved. There was a big Christmas party. This young man came to me and wanted to lead his community group into an experience of giving that really would make an impact on them and on those that they gave to. The Sunday before Christmas, the outreach event happened. This little church plant had nearly 300 people there. The program involved a 30-minute church service, a big lunch, and gift distribution.

Santa and Mrs. Claus were there. Pastor Rick gave the message and nearly one third of the crowd stood at the end of the service to pray and receive Christ as their Savior. At the end of the gift distribution, each child took home a gift purchased just for them. When Pastor Rick saw the number of kids, he feared running out of gifts. Isn't it just like our Heavenly Father to have the last gift go to the last child? That's exactly what happened.

What story! What a moment! What a victory for Christ and His church and a victory for those families who were loved and shown the love of God. Generosity connects us with others, and when we engage our hearts into a journey toward generosity, eternity is changed forever.

Generosity Helps Us Invest in What Matters Most

Generosity helps us invest in what matters most. The secret to the success of any business, leader, family, or church is to invest their time, energy, and resources in what truly matters. The secret to fulfillment as a disciple of Jesus Christ is to have a heart devoted to what the Lord is devoted to. In verse 1 Timothy 6:17-19 above, we see this clarity of focus in what matters most.

The admonition is that the life that is truly a life, the life that truly matters, is the life that is:

- Rich in good deeds
- Generous
- Willing to share

It is the life that is laying up heavenly treasure as a firm foundation for the coming age. So, let me ask you, what really matters? Does the way you live and give reflect what this portion teaches?

The Scriptures say that what really matters is the age to come. If you are rich in this present age, if you are truly living your life in such a way as to matter, you will lay up treasure for the age to come.

In Luke 12:15-21 Jesus said these words:

> And he said to them, "Take care, and be on your guard against all covetousness, for one's life does not consist in the abundance of his possessions." And he told them a parable, saying, "The land of a rich man produced plentifully, and he thought to himself, 'What shall I do, for I have nowhere to store my crops?' And he said, 'I will do this: I will tear down my barns and build larger ones, and there I will store all my grain and my goods. And I will say to my soul, "Soul, you have ample goods laid up for many years; relax, eat, drink, be merry."' But God said to him, 'Fool! This night your soul is required of you, and the things you have prepared, whose will they be?' So is the one who lays up treasure for himself and is not rich toward God."

God said to the man, "Fool!" When we live to store up things for ourselves, and aren't generous toward God, we are foolish. We don't have a grasp of what really matters.

The Lord Jesus himself has told us that what matters is incorruptible, cannot be stolen, and cannot rust from the effects of air, water, or oxidation. This may be a challenging word for you, but don't read this because you think I want something from you. Understand, I want something for you.

Nehemiah wanted the people of Jerusalem to feel safe and secure. He didn't want them mocked any longer. He wanted something for them so they could be free. It wasn't based on what he wanted from them.

Generosity Frees our Hearts

The fourth truth about generosity is that it frees our hearts. In Matthew 6:24, Jesus said,

> "No one can serve two masters, for either he will hate the one and love the other, or he will be devoted to the one and despise the other. You cannot serve God and money."

Jesus had so much to say about money, and its competition for our hearts. You see money is not neutral. It can become your master and it is in direct competition for our hearts with God. Chip Ingram says:

> "Money is the mirror of our heart before God. If you want an accurate measure of your relationship with God, take a look at your checkbook and credit card statements. Notice where your money is going and that will tell you what you are devoted to."[33]

When we engage our pocketbooks toward what God says matters, we are proclaiming to Him that He has our hearts.

REFLECTION QUESTIONS:

1. In the last 10 days, how have you been:

- Rich in good deeds
- Generous
- Willing to share?

2. When you hear about generosity as a value that should mark the life of a Christian, how does that make you feel? Do you agree with it? Does it make you nervous? What thoughts come to you about your finances when you hear the call to generosity?

3. What does a generous life look like to you?

4. Are you willing to use your resources to fight for the future of your church? How can you use your resources to be a builder of the Kingdom of God?

5. What are ways you are pursuing generosity at home? How might this impact your marriage? How might it impact your relationship with your children?

6. Beyond giving to the church and at home, how might you pursue a generous life in our community?

CHAPTER 10

Fighting for Restoration: The Power of Partnership

When something is broken, those most affected are the ones who need to be lifted. This is true at the individual level as well as when you are trying to lift your city. On an individual level, I want to share with you Carolyn's fight story. It's one of pain physically and emotionally. After the loss of her beloved husband, she suffered an injury and spent much of 2018 in a bed. She writes:

> 2018: My 63-year-old husband, Frank, suddenly and unexpectedly, passed away. Five weeks later, while finishing the set-up of our daughter, Claire's, first classroom, and pressing on through the raw grief of our loss, I fell and broke my leg. The next day, as a friend was taking me to meet with a surgeon, I fell off my crutches, breaking three more bones and extending the original break. It was now time to call 911!

Days later, after my surgery, I began my thirteen week stay in what we affectionately refer to as "the home" – where I could be assisted with my daily needs. Almost seven weeks into recovery, my X-ray technician described my deep vein thrombosis as the "biggest she'd ever seen" (not really a desirable distinction). What followed was a "stat" hospital admission, more tests, and IV therapy (all 4 broken bones taken into consideration!).

The morning after I returned to "the home" from the hospital, my mom called to tell me that my dad had suffered a stroke and was hospitalized in Houston. A second one would occur 17 days later.

Twenty weeks after this "life challenge" began, and fourteen weeks after my fall, I was able to go back home with a wheelchair, walker, and lots of physical therapy.

As I look back, I see that 2018 was a year of God's providence and provision. I literally smile as I recount this time. Why?

- Because my God never let go of my right hand (Isaiah 41:13). He held it every day before my husband's death, He held it every minute of every day through my days of challenge and through my mundane ones, and he holds it every day, still. My faith is safe with and well placed in Him. He almost physically lifted me and Claire and carried us through. (John 16:33, Psalm 91:4)

- Because He surrounded both of us, with his angels EVERY SINGLE DAY. They came, within hours of Frank's passing with help, food, and prayer. They were our hands and feet, attending to details we couldn't anticipate or weren't even aware they were taking care of. These angels helped us pull together to get Claire's first day as a teacher off to a sweet and poignant start. They came to emergency rooms, waiting rooms (for both my dad and me), hospital rooms, and doctor's offices for four months. They changed their schedules to help, to spend the night with the "broken" me, to advocate for me, and even to get a little pushy when they needed to. They were prayer warriors and partners, carrying us through the long night of Frank's passing and all the way to complete healing for me and Claire's first months without her dad and in a new job.

Every day for over 150 days, angels looked in on us or looked after me. Who "drops by" a nursing home? The Lord's angels! – on grocery runs, on their way to pick up children from school, on their way to or from the movies, to bring by a cone of soft yogurt, to bring a lunch or dinner to share in my room, to bring flowers or magazines I might like, to wheel me around in the wheelchair, or to just hang out for a few minutes. I believe the Lord poured out His love and care through every single act of those who came, called, laughed, cried, ran my errands or even just thought of us. They embodied the literal hands and feet of Jesus, these godly angels of mine. Every day of that time held a blessing and a joy. (James 1:2-3, Psalm 118:24)

The Lord and I spent our days and nights together in a single room, sparsely furnished, but filled with conversation between us. There was scripture, devotionals, prayer, praise, singing, and listening. (1 Thess. 5:16 – 18, Romans 12:12)

My thoughts were:

- I believed the Lord wanted to get my attention.
- He had something to say that I needed to focus on.
- He wanted my prayers and praises.
- He wanted to reassure and remind me that He is sovereign (Psalm 147: 3-5).
- He wanted me to experience and know how each thought and act of kindness has an impact.
- I was abundantly blessed.
- I was amazed that the number of Frank's days had been fewer than I'd expected (Job 14:15, Psalm 139:16, Psalm 39:4).

- The joy I want to show every day in some small way can be found on even the saddest of days.
- He was preparing me for the seasons that have followed that one.

I did not think I was being punished, nor did I think "why me." Instead, I tend to think, "Why NOT me?"

Through this season, Jesus reminded me gently and humbly, that every gesture matters. The Lord wants me to do more and be better. It matters if I pray, send a card, hold a hand, share a laugh, call, text, email, and spend one minute or one hour visiting. What I do and say can impact others facing a challenge. The Lord gives me those opportunities. He honors, and is honored by, my obedience to Him – to be there, being willing to take the time and act.

What a fight story! I've had the privilege to walk with this sweet lady and her family through these valleys. I can say, her disposition is one of true contentment in Jesus. What's so compelling to me is the way the body of Christ gathered around her and Claire to fill gaps, meet needs, and keep her going. That beautiful picture of partnership is exactly how Jerusalem's walls and gates were restored.

LINKING ARMS

Linking arms carries with it great potential. Unfortunately, in ministry, so many leaders don't take the time to get to know one another or to serve one another. As I came along in ministry, rarely did I see the church and para-church ministry working together in concert. Instead, there was what appeared to be a spirit of competition with one another instead of partnership together. Nehemiah 6:15 tells the story of linking arms together.

So the wall was finished on the twenty-fifth day of the month Elul, in fifty-two days.

Because the people of God were willing to link their arms together, they accomplished so much more for their city than they could have on their own. If the church longs for its people to be generous, its leadership must also strive to be generous with other leaders and organizations within the city. Standing together as kingdom partners enables the linking of arms and an efficiency of use of resource that will help every gift go further.

In December 2017, the seed for the CityRise Network was born in a classroom at a Senior Pastor's Roundtable hosted by the Vanderbloemen Search Group. Thom Rainer, at the time, the CEO of Lifeway Christian Resources, spent a day pouring into this small group of pastors. As he forecasted future things, he talked about the emergence of networks as a key to build health and ministry viability. He discussed his burden for the revitalization of churches and a replanting movement that he was hoping to be a part of. In March 2018, while on a spring break ski trip with my family, I woke up early one morning and could not sleep. I began to see a platform of ministry that entailed mutual collaboration.

The heart of the CityRise Network is the desire to move away from being the hub of a wheel where spokes reach out from us to our partners to being on a platform together where city lifters can collaborate through mutual service. This can only happen when we are in relationship with one another. We see each other on a frequent basis. It's the ride sharing of kingdom impact. Just like you can ride with a ride-sharing service or drive for the ride-sharing service, the CityRise Network is a platform of mutual collaboration where those working for the greater good of the city, can link arms and give to or receive from one another. This new model is the model of collaboration, where leaders of the church and non-profits are in relationship to one another, where they come together for encouragement, relationship and mutual service. The emergence of the network calls for the walls of competition in the Kingdom to be torn down, and for new avenues of partnership to emerge. This is the only way we will be able to lift our cities in each of these areas.

HOW THE GODHEAD FUNCTIONS

When I finished my doctoral work in 2006, I was writing about pastoral leadership. In particular, I was studying the theological foundation of the subordinate leader of the local church, as a follow up to my book, Leading from the Second Chair. In my studies, I was moved deeply by the "economy of God," or the means by which the godhead functions in perfect love and unity. What follows is an excerpt from my doctoral thesis that helps us understand the idea of mutual collaboration, mutual subordination, or mutual service.

> The Father, Son, and Spirit have always been co-eternal. Yet, administratively, there is a clear demonstration of procession and the granting of authority within the Godhead. Bruce Ware states, "Rightful places of authority are respected in Scripture, and the greatest example of this is God the Father."[34] Jesus made this clear in John 5:19 when He said, "The Son can do nothing by himself; he can do only what he sees his Father doing, because whatever the Father does the Son also does."[35]
>
> To be exact, for the purposes of this theological foundation the idea of subordination and granting of authority found in the Godhead pertain only to the administrative relationship of the Godhead. Wayne Grudem terms this administrative distinction as "economic subordination" in which the Son and Spirit are "equal in being but subordinate in role."[36] This idea is central to the doctrine of the Trinity and was first affirmed in the Nicene Creed.[37] Ware states of the relationship of the Father and Son, "The Son in fact is the eternal Son of the eternal Father, and hence, the Son stands in relationship of eternal submission under the authority of His Father."[38]
>
> **Jesus' Claims of Subordination and Authority**
> Being the source of all authority, God the Father granted all authority to the Son to accomplish through His atonement and establishment of the church the redemptive purposes of

the Father.[39] Having received this authority from the Father, Jesus fulfilled the task that the Father sent Him to accomplish.

The Son and the Spirit

Jesus gave the gift of the Holy Spirit, the gifts of grace to the individual members of the church body and also appointed officers to the church so that those in His body[40] might be governed and equipped for the works of service and the building of His body.[41] This is all to be accomplished through the leading and empowering of the indwelling Holy Spirit.

It must be noted that Jesus and the Holy Spirit practice mutual submission to one another in order to complete the task that the Father gave to Jesus. Clearly, Jesus accomplished all that He accomplished by following the Holy Spirit,[42] being full of the Holy Spirit and being led by the Spirit.[43] William Evans states, "How dependent Jesus Christ was, in His state of humiliation, on the Holy Spirit! If He needed to depend solely upon the Spirit, can we afford to do less?" [44] In summation, Evans says of Jesus that He was conceived by and born of the Spirit (Luke 1:35); led by the Spirit (Matt 4:1); anointed by the Spirit for service (Acts 10:38); crucified in the power of the Spirit (Heb 9:14); raised by the power of the Spirit (Rom 1:4, 8:11). [45]

Yet, the Spirit was also subordinate to the Son. The doctrine of double procession teaches that the Spirit proceeded both from the Father and the Son. This comes from John 15:26 which states, "When the Counselor comes, whom I will send to you from the Father, the Spirit of truth who goes out from the Father, he will testify about me." [46]

The Trinity, Authority and Subordination

What should one conclude about the nature and characteristics of the Trinity at this point? First, it should be concluded that God the Father is the source of ultimate authority and Jesus and the Holy Spirit, the source of subordination. Or, more forcefully, to be God the Father is to be in authority and share authority. To be God the Son or God the Spirit is to be in subordination to the Father and mutually to one another. Ware goes so far as to say, "It is the nature of God both to exert authority and to obey in submission. And since this is the eternal nature of God, we may know that it is beautiful and it is good." [47]

Second, the persons of the Trinity grant authority to completely fulfill the redemptive mission of God. This takes place as God the Father grants all authority to Jesus. Jesus then grants authority to the Spirit to lead, empower, and accomplish the task of redemption that is to be accomplished through the church.

Third, the Trinitarian model of authority, subordination, the granting of authority, and mutual subordination has important implications for lead leaders and subordinate leaders in the local church. These principles are modeled by the Godhead and should be understood and applied to the relationships of authority and subordination in believers' lives. [48]

I would apologize for the theology lesson, but I'm not really sorry. You see, if this is the way the Father, Son, and Holy Spirit live out unity in their Kingdom, shouldn't it be the way we, as the people of God also live out unity on earth? We pray, "Your kingdom come, your will be done, on earth as it is in heaven," but we live miles apart in competition with one another.

If we want to bring God's kingdom on earth as it is in heaven, then the people of God in government, education, business, entertainment, sports, media, and the church/para-church should work to collaborate together, maximizing opportunity and influence to go to the broken and lift them. What happened to Carolyn on the micro-level, leaders in these major sectors could be doing on the macro-level.

HELPING OUR CITY RISE

In spring 2018, we established a number of vision teams. One team worked on the idea of the network. We had gone through the branding process to create the umbrella brand called CityRise, then through a series of meetings and conversations, we created a game plan by which we hope to lift our city and world by generously giving the gospel of Jesus Christ.

Here is the overarching framework of the plan put together by the CityRise Network Expansion Team:

> We believe that there are more people throughout this amazing city who want to build on foundations, connect their purpose to impact, and long to do more together, but they don't yet know the living Christ. It's time for us to truly position ourselves to reach them. They too have been created for greater, but it will take a strategic network, aligning our gifts, resources, and partnerships to reach them for Christ.
>
> The CityRise Network is a collaboration of churches and ministries rooted in the local church to provide a platform of partnership and act as a conduit which…
>
> - creates opportunity for church expansion,
> - convenes leaders and ministries,
> - cares for leaders' health and wellbeing,
> - carries administrative burdens,
> - catalyzes growth for the kingdom.
>
> The CityRise Network is created for kingdom growth and expansion in a climate of vast change. By identifying and cultivating opportunities in the greater Houston area, the network connects areas where the kingdom is thriving and flourishing to areas where the kingdom witness is dormant or diminishing. Through collaborative church and ministry partnerships, the

CityRise Network will see sustainability, growth and expansion of God's ministry.

Upon a 90-year foundational commitment to the local church, love of the gospel message, and a heritage of missions, we will build a network of churches and ministries. We will continue to love our city by investing deeply, leading wisely, and expecting greater things to come. We are positioned to build this CityRise Network and advance the kingdom in our city because of our rich history, talent base, and gifting.

We will be a network compelled to progress the gospel. We recognize the risks associated when venturing out, we must discern and be disciplined about the opportunities which are appropriate, but the risk is greater if we wait for opportunities to come to us. If we only look inward, we lose sight of the stewardship of the great commission. Frankly, we believe that eternal reward is at risk for our church, and eternity is at risk for those we are called to reach.

CityRise is driven by our conviction to reach those who have not yet believed. We know there are others in our area who feel the same. Let's join to build a network that advances God's kingdom in our city.

THE ONGOING TASK

When the books of Ezra and Nehemiah close, there is the sense that, though so much was accomplished in the rebuilding of the temple and the walls of Jerusalem, there was an ongoing task of leading the people to be the called out, separate people, who belong to the Lord. There were moments of great reform and renewal. There was repentance from sin, restoration, and then the repeating of the same old mistakes. It's the story of the life of an imperfect people. But no longer did their walls lie in ruin. No longer were they a laughing-stock to the other nations. The coming generations had an opportunity for something far greater because Zerubbabel, Joshua, Ezra and Nehemiah were weighed down by burden and compelled to attempt something that could only be done with God's help. It's an amazing fight story, and one that helps inform ours.

If you find yourself in the fight of your life, keep in mind, that the one who helped these leaders of old is available to help you. Press into Him, trust Him, and allow Him to have his way. He won't waste the pain, whether you are fighting for yourself, your family, your church or your city. To reinforce this point one more time, let me share with you a concluding fight story from Cameron. He's an emergency room physician at one of our hospitals in the Texas Medical Center.

> I'm happy to share my fight story. I focus on round 1 because there have been a couple more since. But once Jesus leads you through round 1, you're not really all that concerned about the rest. After all, if God is for us, who can be against us?

> The last year of my critical care fellowship came with a surprise. My wife of four years no longer loved me and was leaving. We were not believers, but I recall the shock and horror of realizing her love was not unconditional. Admittedly, I hadn't been a good husband. I worked too much and didn't value her as a man should. Nonetheless, this was quite unexpected and marked the first time in my life that anything major hadn't gone according to my plan. This was the first time I realized I wasn't God.

> In the months that followed, my broken heart led to so many blessings. I learned that I was broken yet lovable. In the process, I learned to love so many others who I had arrogantly dismissed in the past. I learned I didn't need to have all the answers because God did. He had a plan for me which was better than mine. I learned how transformative unconditional love is and how to apply it to my next and most important relationships (I'm now married with three kids). I learned to have humility and a calm confidence based on faith in Jesus not my own works.

> Round 1 of my fight left me with a broken nose and a few scars. But a couple years later when I rushed into round 2, I

was equipped with a peace that comes from knowing the Lord. Round 2 gave me some new scars but also earned my freedom from sexual addiction and shame. Round 3 led to the recognition of how wonderful it is to be slow to anger and abounding in steadfast love. I have no idea how many more rounds lie ahead. It doesn't matter. I'm going to finish this fight well. Jesus is in my corner.

Amen! As we conclude our time together, allow me to encourage you in the fight. Notice the encouragement of the Apostle Paul to Timothy. 1 Timothy 6:12 states:

> Fight the good fight of the faith. Take hold of the eternal life to which you were called and about which you made the good confession in the presence of many witnesses.

As we seek to be faithful with this life, may Paul's confession of 2 Timothy 4:7 be ours as well.

> I have fought the good fight, I have finished the race, I have kept the faith.

REFLECTION QUESTIONS:

1. How does Carolyn's story resonate with you? Have you been in her position, or have you had the privilege of serving someone in this position? What did you learn from that experience?

2. In what ways are you serving at your church? Is this a priority for you? Are you a volunteer that others can count on so that the church can function well?

3. Did understanding how the God-head functions assist you in seeing how you might contribute to unity in the church? Might it also help you see the potential in how churches and para-church organizations might work together?

4. What are some of the biggest constraints to partnership in ministry that you see? How might these be lifted?

5. The ongoing task is great. How might you take what you have learned through this study and live differently?

Acknowledgements

A project of this magnitude would not be possible without the support of so many. I'm afraid to list these people out, as I might miss someone. But I want to take the time to say thank you for your support and belief in the message I sensed the Lord giving me.

First, to my wife, Julee, thank you for your constant devotion to our Lord, His church and our family. You are such a gift to me and to so many. You get up every day and fight for others, with our family at the top of the list of those you are fighting for. To my kids, Brady, Cooper, and Carson, you are such a joy to parent. You make me proud to be called your father. To the CityRise Executive Council: You all are such a gift to me. Thank you Ed, Harry, Brad, Steve, Lorraine, Jan, David, Tony, Mark, Stephanie, Liana, and Kirby for your constant encouragement and belief in me and the church. You all love to move the kingdom forward!

To the people of CityRise, including the congregations at West University Baptist, Crosspoint Church-Bellaire, CityRise Missouri City, Iglesia Crosspoint, West U Chinese Church, CityRise Emmanuel, and all of our network parnters, you all are such a blessing to me. Thank you for putting up with me for so many years and for your continued support, encouragement, and pursuit of the vision to lift our city and world by generously giving the gospel of Jesus Christ.

To Brent and Cassie Gallagher, thank you for inviting me to grab the rope. I'll never be the same! To Dan Hall, I am who I am today because you poured so much of your journey into me. I love you my brother! Heavy Weight Champ, Lou Savarese, the use of your gym to film our small group curriculum was amazing. Thank you for making that available. You have always been a blessing to me!

To our staff, you are a great team who loves Jesus and can't wait to take the next hill for His glory. Thank you for serving alongside me in such tumultuous times. A special thank you to Laura Hatfield and Antonetta Russo for allowing me to constantly bounce ideas off of you. To Jennifer Dean, thanks for pushing on me early on in the process.

To Brett, Pam, Allen, and the LifeTogether team, thank you for helping me refine and shape this message. It's so much fun to work with you and I can't wait for even greater things that are yet to come.

To my Lord Jesus, thank you for your amazing grace. I pray that you are glorified by this project!

May we continue to stay expectant of greater things that are yet to come!

Roger Patterson

October, 2021

NOTES

INTRODUCTION

1. Alan Platt, City Changers: Being the Presence of Christ in Your Community, David C. Cook, 2017, p.160.

2. Alan Platt, City Changers: Being the Presence of Christ in Your Community, David C. Cook, 2017, p.13.

CHAPTER 1

3. Elwell, W. A., & Beitzel, B. J. (1988). Cyrus the Great. In Baker encyclopedia of the Bible (Vol. 1, p. 565). Grand Rapids, MI: Baker Book House.

4. Wiersbe, W. W. (1993). Wiersbe's Expository Outlines on the Old Testament (Ezr 1–2). Wheaton, IL: Victor Books.

CHAPTER 2

5. Wiersbe, W. W. (1993). Wiersbe's Expository Outlines on the Old Testament (Ne 1–3). Wheaton, IL: Victor Books.

6. Platt, City Changers, 163-165.

7. White, R. E. O. (1988). Lord. In Baker encyclopedia of the Bible (Vol. 2, p. 1346). Grand Rapids, MI: Baker Book House.

CHAPTER 3

8. https://www.adaa.org/understanding-anxiety/depression

9. Go to www.wellevations.com to take Dr. Frey's assessment. There is a fee associated, but you will also have an opportunity to engage with a professional coach in any of these areas to get you moving forward to make progress.

CHAPTER 4

10. Matthew 6:21.

11. Timothy Keller with Kathy Keller, The Meaning of Marriage, (Dutton: New York, New York), p. 223-224.

CHAPTER 5

12. https://www.agapedevelopment.org/about/our-story

13. Jamieson, R., Fausset, A. R., & Brown, D. (1997). Commentary Critical and Explanatory on the Whole Bible (Vol. 1, p. 385). Oak Harbor, WA: Logos Research Systems, Inc.

14. Breneman, M. (1993). Ezra, Nehemiah, Esther (electronic ed., Vol. 10, pp. 78–79). Nashville: Broadman & Holman Publishers.

15. Wiersbe, W. W. (1993). Wiersbe's Expository Outlines on the Old Testament (Ezr). Wheaton, IL: Victor Books.

CHAPTER 6

16. Wiersbe, W. W. (1996). The Bible Exposition Commentary (Vol. 2, pp. 56–57). Wheaton, IL: Victor Books.

SECTION 3

17. John Piper, Let the Nations Be Glad, (Baker Academic: Grand Rapids), 2010, p.30.

18. Ibid., p. 81.

19. Piper, pp. 94-98. Piper does an extensive treatment of the topic of the glory of God throughout the Scriptures, including the ministry of Jesus and the ministry of the Holy Spirit. He ends this section in quoting Jonathan Edward's book titled, The Dissertation Concerning the End for Which God Created the World. Edwards says, "The great end of God's works, which is so variously expressed in the Scripture, is indeed but ONE; and this one end is most properly and comprehensively called, THE GLORY OF GOD."

CHAPTER 7

20. Breneman, M. (1993). Ezra, Nehemiah, Esther (electronic ed., Vol. 10, p. 92). Nashville: Broadman & Holman Publishers.

21. Ibid, p.91.

22. Piper, Let the Nations Be Glad, p. 87.

23. https://www.tandfonline.com/doi/full/10.1080/24735132.2020.1731203

24. Platt, City Changers, p. 77.

CHAPTER 8

25. Breneman, M. (1993). Ezra, Nehemiah, Esther (electronic ed., Vol. 10, p. 97). Nashville: Broadman & Holman Publishers.

26. Wiersbe, W. W. (1993). Wiersbe's Expository Outlines on the Old Testament (Ezr). Wheaton, IL: Victor Books.

27. Breneman, M. (1993). Ezra, Nehemiah, Esther (electronic ed., Vol. 10, pp. 178–179). Nashville: Broadman & Holman Publishers.

28. Patterson, Roger, A Minute of Vision for Men: 365 Motivational Moments to Kick-Start Your Day, (Tyndale House Publishers: Carol Stream), p. 276.

SECTION 4

29. Platt, 77.

30. Platt, p. 73.

CHAPTER 9

31. Gordon MacDonald, Generosity: Moving Toward a Life that is Truly Life, Generous Church, 2009.

32. These principles that head this section on generosity come from Chip Ingram's work, The Genius of Generosity, pp. 15-20.

33. Ingram, p. 20.

CHAPTER 10

34. Ware, Father, Son, and Holy Spirit, 65-6.

35. John 5:19, NIV.

36. Wayne Grudem, Systematic Theology: An Introduction to Biblical Doctrine (Leicester: Inter-Varsity Press and Zondervan, 1994), 251.

37. Ibid.

38. Ware, Father, Son, and Holy Spirit, 71.

39. See John 17:2; Matt 28:18; Eph 1:22.

40. See Eph 4:7; Rom 12:6-8; 1 Cor 12:4-11.

41. See Eph 4:11-12; Acts 14:23; 20:17; Titus 1:5; 1 Pet 5:1-2.

42. See Isa 11:1-2 and Ware, Father, Son, and Holy Spirit, 88.

43. Luke 4:1-2.

44. William Evans, The Great Doctrines of the Bible (Chicago: Moody Press, 1980), 119.

45. Ibid.

46. John 15:26, NIV.

47. Ware, Father, Son, and Holy Spirit, 85.

48. Roger Patterson, The Theological Foundation of the Subordinate Leader of the Local Church, pp.14-22, 2006.

Original Song Lyrics

FIGHT FOR YOU

You fought for me

You fought when I was blind, but now I see
I'm rescued, redeemed, never forsaken
You lifted me up from the ruins of my own making
Pulled my heart from deepest deep
Raised to walk in your victory

So when I stand up and put my hands up
I will sing your victory, O my God
And when I'm knocked down
I'm still on your ground
And I know where my soul is found
When I fight for you

God if I am strong, then I will fight for the weak
If I am not, then I will fight down on my knees
I gotta fight to believe I gotta fight to be true
Yeah sometimes I gotta fight just to find my way back to you

And you are never too far away, never too far away
You are never too far away when I speak your name
You are never too far away, never too far away
You are never too far away when I speak your name

Jesus, Jesus
You are never too far away when I speak your name
Jesus, Jesus You are never too far away when I speak your name

About the Author

Dr. Roger Patterson is the Senior Pastor for CityRise, a network of churches and ministries committed to lifting our city and our world by generously giving the gospel of Jesus Christ. CityRise includes campuses in and around the greater Houston, Texas area. He has held the role of Senior Pastor since 2010.

Roger graduated from Houston Baptist University in 1995 with a degree in Speech Communication and Christianity and attended Southwestern Baptist Theological Seminary where he received his Master of Divinity in 1998 and Doctor of Ministry Degree in 2006. With over fifteen years of experience in the subordinate leadership role in the local church, Roger coauthored Leading from the Second Chair with his friend and colleague Mike Bonem. Roger has extensive experience in training other leaders, whether they are in the first or second chair, to understand the dynamics of what it looks like to lead and to follow.

Roger is also the author A Minute of Vision for Men, a 365-day devotional guide aimed at bolstering men's lives by helping them determine God's vision and purpose for their lives.

Roger and his wife, Julee, have been married for 26 years and have three children: Brady, Cooper, and Carson. Roger loves to coach his kids' sports teams, play golf, hunt, and spend time with his family.